Praise for *Tho*

M000012111

"Whether you whine about the weather, rage about your age, or complain about getting on a plane, January Jones has some wise, witty, and wonderful solutions for whatever you have on your whine list."

— Allen Klein, Author
The Healing Power of Humor and *WorkLaughs*

"January Jones is so hilarious! She illuminates why whining is such a problem in our lives. As a Law of Attraction Coach, I know how important it is to focus on what you appreciate instead of what you depreciate. Whining is depreciating at its best and will always attract more negative people, situations, and problems to you. Way to go, January."

— Christy Whitman, Author, Speaker, Law of Attraction Coach

"*Thou Shalt Not Whine* is hilarious and only too true. January Jones delightfully points out our common foibles and then helps us overcome them with wit, grace, and a keen eye for the telling detail. A lot of fun to read, fast and snappy; this one has 'bestseller' written all over it!"

— Patricia Kokinos, Author
Angel Park: A Novel

"*Thou Shalt Not Whine* is a wonderful book! Even though January Jones is nicer than Dr. Laura and prettier than Dr. Phil, she still made me see another side in me. I had to admit that I too can be a Whiner! I had to laugh about her husband and all the pillows though, because I too can't understand all the pillows—especially the ones we're not allowed to use! I blame it all on HGTV! But here I go whining again! Only now I catch myself and smile. I think I'm gonna go out and buy another pillow for our bed!"

— Joe Sindoni, Author
50 Reasons Not To Have Kids

"January Jones's book is a delightful exposé on just how focused we have become on 'not enough.' This is an attitude that stops us from counting our blessings and ultimately creating a preferred reality. From whining about your losing sports team to planes that arrive late, Ms. Jones reminds us that we always have the option to keep that Eleventh Commandment and subsequently cause ourselves to be happier and healthier. A delightful must read!"

— Elfreda Pretorius, Author
Stop Struggling and Start Living:
The Rules of the Game

"*Thou Shalt Not Whine* is a thoughtful and lighthearted look at whining and how we can shift it to smiling. The world will never run out of the need for this kind of hopeful message!"

— Elizabeth Diane & Andrew Marshall, Authors
Listening with Heart 360:
The New Paradigm for Women

"*Thou Shalt Not Whine* is priceless! It's the perfect gift for anyone who wants to be healthy and happy with humor, honey, and hope...or for people who are just hopeless!"

— John Curtis, Ph.D., Author
Cohabitating

"Next time you feel the urge to complain again, watch out for January Jones! She certainly knows how to take all the fun out of whining. *Thou Shalt Not Whine* is a fun read and great gift to give to your friends, especially those guilty of feeling sorry for themselves. Bravo, January Jones."

— Auriela McCarthy, Author
The Power of the Possible

Thou Shalt Not Whine
The Eleventh Commandment

**What we whine about, why we do it and
how to stop**

*Successimo
2 u !*

**Compiled & Written
by
January Jones**

*January
ones*

**Beaufort Books
New York**

Thou Shalt Not Whine

The Eleventh Commandment

BEAUFORT
BOOKS

Beaufort Books, Inc.
27 West 20th St.
New York, NY 10011
www.beaufortbooks.com

Library of Congress Cataloging-in-Publication Data

Jones, January, 1978-
  Thou shalt not whine, the eleventh commandment : what we whine about, why we do it and how to stop / compiled & written by January Jones.
     p. cm.
  ISBN 978-0-8253-0579-5 (alk. paper)
  1. Conduct of life--Humor. 2. Human behavior--Humor. I. Title.

  PN6231.C6142J66 2008
  818'.5402--dc22

                            2008016928

This book is intended for education and/or entertainment purposes only. Readers suffering from depression or stress-related illnesses should use their own judgment or consult a medical expert or their own physicians for specific applications to their individual situations.

Printed in the United States of America.

In memory of my grandmothers,
Mary & Johanna

They taught me about whining and winning.

Contents

Foreword

Everybody whines; just look around you wherever you go. We are currently experiencing a worldwide epidemic of whining, and it is only getting worse as the world throws more our way to whine about every day: terrorists, corporate raiders, the housing slump, the shrinking economy, expensive wars, ineffectual government, the hair-raising price of gas, cellulite, acid reflux, the effects of saturated fats. Everybody whines because everybody seems to have something to whine about these days. But just because it's natural doesn't mean it's nice, and I'm here to put an end to it.

My name is January Jones, and I am the Whine Tester. Welcome to my book, and to my crusade to rid the world of this toxic, easily curable habit for once and for all.

Have you ever wondered why so many people are constantly whining about this or that? Do you incessantly have to deflect the negative energy people spew by whining all around you? Have you ever wanted to tell them to just shut up and keep it to themselves? Has anyone near and dear to you driven you crazy with their whining and complaining? Have you ever asked yourself what they are *really* whining about? And have you ever wondered how to stop them—or, if whining is your own weakness—how to stop yourself?

Perhaps you don't believe me. There are skeptics. Perhaps you think people are actually getting mellower and mellower as we evolve. In this case, indulge me by conducting a little experiment that has already proven successful in waking other doubters up to this growing problem. Don't worry, it's easy: simply keep your ears open next time you go out to do a series of errands about town. The retail arena is the prime sector of society for everyday whine cultivation and practice, as pointed out to me by one of my many survey subjects, whose own moment of revelation about the insidious prevalence of public whining went like this:

> *You were right! The other day while I was out and about running my usual boring errands, I noticed that everywhere I went, people were whining, and wondered why I hadn't*

noticed it before. While I was at Whole Foods, one woman was whining about the express self-service check out being too slow—and it was! Next stop, I found myself in the long, gray line at the post office, and every single person there was whining, whether it was a loud "Come on!", a forceful sigh or a simple rolling of the eyes. After that it was on to the gas station, where the outrageous prices were causing a spontaneous whine fest among the self-serve customers at my island. I tried to resist, but I couldn't help joining in...

I have since successfully helped this complainer and many others to stop whining and start winning instead, and I am hoping this book will help you to do the same. Now, you may be asking, "What makes this January Jones person one of the world's foremost experts on whining?" And right you are to do so. I hold no degrees in psychology or sociology, but my experience has been more valuable and useful than any mere degree could have been. First of all, I used to suffer from the whining disease myself. Like most girls, I was born a natural whiner. I knew how to get just about anything I wanted by whining, and I quickly mastered all the standard whining tactics while creating some new ones along the way.

My second qualification is that I'm a woman, which means that I can be anything I want to be—and change my mind about what that is whenever I feel like it. Currently I am a golfer, a writer, a wife, a widow, a mother and a grandmother. Also, I host a radio show and publish a weekly e-zine called *Whine Time*. When it comes to whining, nobody does it better or knows how to stop it more effectively than I do.

As the Whine Tester, I have come up with my own "theories" to aid in my research and whine therapy. I would love to share with all my readers my Grand *Whinestein* Theory. Granted, it's not as paradigm-shattering, nor do I believe it will remain as timeless, as Einstein's Theory of Relativity, which we all know comes down to the eloquent $e=mc^2$ (even if we have no idea what it means). I am not now nor have I ever been a scientist, and I know it is presumptuous of me to even write about Albert Einstein, but I had no choice. A skeptic once said that I had as much chance of writing a book about whining as I had of writing a book about Einstein. So, non-believer, wherever you now may be, here it is just for you. I'm now writing about whining and Einstein, all in one book—and on one page, no less. Einstein explained space and time to us through high science, and I now offer my own humble findings on the folk science of the whine:

January Jones's Whinestein Theory

$$W=MC^2$$
(Whining = Major Complaining, squared)

In order to expand upon this theory, I developed a technique for diagnosing severity of dysfunction and prescribing curative therapy. My Four Star "A" rating system is designed to help both victims and verbalizers to recognize and address this epidemic.

★ **Annoying—causing mild anger or impatience.**
Intention of Perpetrator:
I just want to complain and get sympathy.

★★ **Attention-hording—requiring unwilling mental focus and causing strong impatience.**
Intention of Perpetrator:
You WILL acknowledge me, NOW.

★★★ **Aggravating—causing severe anger or irritation that can lead to rage.**
Intention of Perpetrator:
I really want to drive you CRAZY!

★ ★ ★ ★ **Abusive—causing psychological harm or worse through thorough insult and offense.***

Intention of Perpetrator:
I will not stop until I have irreparably damaged you by verbal attack....

*NOTE: Abusive whining is a serious problem and I don't like to deal with or validate it in any way, shape or form. If you feel that you or someone you know is a victim of abusive whining, please call a psychoanalyst or the proper authorities.

Now I'd like to share with you how my stop-whining system, and this book, works. There are twelve chapters, each one dealing with the top ten whines you are likely to hear from a certain part of your community or family, followed by how to deal with them.

To give you a vivid example, here I'm going to let you in on a whining problem that I have been dealing with throughout my long, long marriage. In this book, you can find this specific whine and its associated cures in Chapter Four (Couples), and it is this, more than anything, that has made me the truly well-versed expert I am today:

My husband is a Three-Star Pillow Whiner. This may not seem like much of a problem to you, but let me tell you about it. It started out as a simple One-Star Annoying Whine. We'd go to bed at night and he would start throwing the pillows from the bed on the floor. "Why do we have so many pillows? I need one and you need one. Why are there ten pillows on our bed?" Now, this was something I could ignore since wives are good at ignoring husbands.

Very soon, though, he became a Two-Star Pillow Whiner. He wanted attention, and he knew just how to get it: he went *public!* I couldn't believe it. There we were out to dinner with another couple, and my husband leans over to casually ask the other husband, "How many pillows do you have on your bed?" Well, the other man had no idea and he had to ask his wife. Pretty soon, we were all having pillow talk...in *public!*

Then my husband went over the top by turning into a Three-Star Whiner on the spot. Once the other husband had ascertained the pillow count on their bed from his wife—which, my husband pointed out with a raised eyebrow to me, was a smaller number than so annoyingly inhabited our own bed—my husband came out with this: "Tell me, are you ever allowed to touch the pillows?" I was flabbergasted, but he went on: "Are you allowed to take them off at night or put them back on the bed in the morning? And if you dare to, don't they always turn out to be put back the *wrong way*?!"

The other wife and I shared a copasetic glance that included not only sympathy for our shared lot as women, but solidarity in the unassailable fact that no man on earth has ever or ever will put the pillows back on the bed well enough to please his wife.

How do you deal with a Three-Star Pillow Whiner? In this case, I have used the Universal Smile Cure to great success. It is done with a sincere smile and goes like this: "Honey, how about if we go out for a romantic dinner tonight?" This is followed by, "Sweetie, if you promise not to discuss our bedroom pillows anymore with other men, after dinner we can cuddle in front of the fireplace for our own pillow talk," Then you can finish up with, "Who knows, maybe we can count the pillows together as we toss them on the floor, and then you'll know for sure how many we have." Well, you get the idea! Everyone agrees that smiling is better than whining.

While smiling is universal, though, it's not everyone who can crack a winning smile at will. Smiling is something that some people are born doing while others can't be taught to do it. I'm one of those born to smile, while my husband only smiles as a last resort. One time our family auditioned for the *Family Feud* game show, and my husband had to go to smiling therapy before we could get on. Once we were on stage with Richard Dawson, he couldn't stop smiling. It was a manic, nervous, hysterical, scary smile that none of us is likely to see again, but it was fortunately saved for posterity on home video.

I have the opposite problem in that I can't stop smiling. Once I was even smiling when I came out of the operating room on a stretcher in a semi-conscious state. Life is usually easier for anyone who smiles, but it can create some pitfalls. For example, it can be inappropriate at most funerals. It is difficult when I don't know the bereaved family that well and I'm there smiling like the Sunshine Lady. Church and serious stage plays are also treacherous territories for me to navigate. The problem is that smiles can quickly escalate into hysterical, inappropriate behavior. I can't count the times that I have looked across the aisle connecting with another smiling idiot as we dissolved into uncontrollable laughter.

Despite my own self-inflicted problems with smiling, I still highly recommend it as a cure for whining. Smiling will disarm a whiner every time. It is impossible to whine while returning a smile. True whiners will be torn between whining or ignoring you, either of which would make them rude. And even the most inveterate of whiners knows that being rude is much worse than being a compulsive complainer.

The best thing about the smiling cure is that you can pretty much say or do anything as long as you have a smile on your face. It is one of my favorites, but you will find over 100 cures for over 100 whines in this book to add to your bag of tricks. These cures have been culled from years of personal research along with a survey of several hundred people of different ages, genders, races and social strata.

Whining is a toxic topic that the survey subjects responded to with amazing and revealing honesty and humor. The top ten whines for all age groups are exposed and dealt with in this book, along with cures that work.

Doing this survey has been one of the most enjoyable projects that I have ever undertaken. Each day my e-mail brings me humorous, creative replies from so many people from all over the world that I already have enough whines to fill up a few more volumes. It has been a real education. I feel like I've become Clearing House Central for the complaining and whining in our world; and here, for the first time, I am able to share my experience and findings with you and yours.

I hope you enjoy finding your favorite whiners in the following pages; and if you happen to find yourself, whatever you do, don't whine about it!

Introductory Lesson

Flying without Whining

I begin with airline travel since overcoming whining while zooming through the air has been one of my greatest achievements in life.

I was the first one in my family to ever fly in an airplane, and not too many of them, besides me, have done it to this day, coded as they are with the Whining About Flying DNA glitch. My grandma always said that if God had wanted her to fly, he would have given her wings—and she truly meant it. This wisdom applied to driving for her too. She wasn't born with tires attached to her legs, so she wasn't about to ride in a car!

In 1963, despite my inbred terror, I flew to Miami on Eastern Airlines for an interview to become an airline stewardess. I experienced such an incredible adrenaline rush on takeoff that I was barely able to breathe, let alone talk. In the air, I was thrilled to be defying the Law of Gravity. The landing was a cinch, since by then not only had I somewhat acclimated, but I had been able to drink enough wine to get me down without screaming or making a scene. Long story short, I was hired, but too proud to admit I couldn't fly without whining. Actually I was so desperate to escape my boring life in Detroit that having to fly wasn't enough to stop me.

Doing that job, I simply couldn't whine on pain of dismissal, so I just enacted some recessive stiff-upper-lip gene and smiled through my troubles. Despite my continuing terror, I really wanted to be a stewardess in the worst way, and sometimes I certainly was.

Years later after my first husband was killed during a test flight, I continued to put on a brave front about flying for the sake of my children. Besides, I am addicted to doing things that scare me silly, especially when I am trying to stop whining about life.

To this day, it has been difficult to overcome the urge to indulge in whining while flying, mainly because I never have been able to understand how it all works. No matter how many times my second and current husband, also a pilot, explains to me the mechanics of flight, I still don't get it. I never will be able to comprehend how a 747 airplane that weighs tons can lift off and soar through the skies.

I do, however, have my own theory about how planes work: When I am on a plane during take off and lift my toes upward, the plane will lift up and off without any problems. I don't know if not doing it might cause a crash because I have never, ever *not* done it. I must confess that this is not an original theory but rather one that was passed on to me early in my career. It came my way from an older, wiser and far more experienced stewardess who had already conquered her fear of flying. Upon the announcement of landing, one need only reverse the process and point the toes downward, and the plane will touch down with a comforting, fluid grace.

I can somewhat justify my previous problem of whining while flying because I experienced some really scary moments up in the air as a stewardess: emergency foamed-runway landings, hearing about other fatal accidents while serving cocktails, extreme conditions that made my life flash before my eyes—these were all part of the daily routine in my chosen career; another important part of it was to keep those things from the passengers so that they wouldn't completely freak out

As for being a passenger, what's not to whine about, especially now with increased security, longer delays and an alarming trend for lost baggage? Fortunately, there's no more whining about the poor quality of airline food since actual food is no longer served to those in coach. As Wolfgang Puck once said, "To me, an airplane is a great place to diet."

Over the past few decades, I've considerably decreased the likelihood of my whining about flying because I can almost enjoy it when my pilot husband is in the cockpit. I can even sleep while he's up front because I know that there is someone driving who wants to live as much as I do, if not more.

One of our favorite flights together was when we were invited to land on the aircraft carrier *USS Carl Vinson* in a Navy plane. Once on board, I spent the entire night thinking about being catapulted off the deck the next morning. It was terrifying when it happened, but I didn't whine. I screamed a little as we were shot off the ship but I didn't wet my pants.

It seems my destiny was to fly, to wed fliers and to raise fliers. I have one daughter who is a pilot, two daughters who have been fight attendants and a son who is a non-whining frequent flyer. Even after all these years, I'm still a white-knuckled flier, but at least now I can talk about it. Take it from me: It's possible to be fearful and brave at the same time just *as long as you don't whine about it*!

**When you think about flying, it's nuts really.
Here you are at about 40,000 feet, screaming along at
700 miles an hour and you're sitting there
drinking Diet Pepsi and eating peanuts.
It just doesn't make any sense.**

—David Letterman

Top 10 Whines About
Flying

✈✈✈✈   ✈✈✈✈   ✈✈✈✈

#1   Airports
#2   Reservations
#3   Increased Security
#4   Lost Bags
#5   Jet Lag
#6   Big Crowds, Small Seats
#7   Crying Babies
#8   Turbulence
#9   Flight Delays
#10 Food, or the Lack of it

**If God had really intended men to fly,
He'd have made it easier to get to the airport.**

—George Winters

1
Airports

✈✈✈✈ ✈✈✈✈ ✈✈✈✈

> **There is nothing like an airport for bringing you down to earth.**
>
> —*Robert Gordon*

Whine A: I hate going there.

Why: Unfortunately, airports have become our worst nightmare. They are too crowded, too confusing, too big and too frustrating for the average traveler—whining heaven for the constant complainer. It all begins going downhill when you try to find a parking place or, God forbid, attempt to sit in the arrivals lane for more than two seconds without security chasing you off. And then there are those loud, obnoxious, repetitive Announcements that hound you from all sides, and all those annoying tourists...

Whine B: It's such a mob scene.

Cure: The **"red-eye"** cure is a brutal but effective way of dealing with impossible airports, especially for sound sleepers. Red-eye flights depart around midnight, when all sensible people are at home asleep, and arrive in the early hours of the next day. Red-eye fliers are easy to spot because their eyes are bleary and puffy and bruised-looking, and their clothes look like they have been slept in...because they have. On the other hand, they usually also display a serene smile and immitigable calm for having slept through whatever small amount of whining may have occurred while their eyes were so deliciously busy getting red.

2
Reservations

✈✈✈✈ ✈✈✈✈ ✈✈✈✈

**If god had meant man to fly,
He would have given us tickets.**

—Mel Brooks

Whine A: They always put me on hold.

Why: When you try to make reservations with any airline, it is like navigating a minefield of modern technology—and the people who are there as a last resort to help you with it are even less customer-friendly. As soon as your call goes through, you are put on hold—and then your problems begin. Endlessly circling in a telephonic holding pattern, you wait so long that you forget where you are or where you want to go. The worst part is that you'll never speak to a real person—and it's just not fun complaining to a machine.

Whine B: I hate talking to a machine.

Cure: The **"express easy check-in e-ticket"** cure is a new innovation that has made flying almost bearable. It is quick, easy and enjoyable once you have gone through the initial learning curve; and though it isn't quite instant and doesn't exactly involve the human touch, it is far less time-consuming and alienating than booking airline reservations on the phone with disembodied, oddly cadenced voices that sound only vaguely like real people. With most airlines, you can even print out boarding passes 24 hours before your flight, thus circumventing all human interaction until you have to deal with those fine professionals at security, which is the subject of our next whine.

3
Increased Security

✈✈✈✈ ✈✈✈✈ ✈✈✈✈

**Whenever we land safely in a plane,
we promise God a little something.**

—*Mignon McLaughlin*

Whine A: These lines are too long.

Why: Sadly, ever since 9/11, increased airport security measures in the name of preventing terrorism have made traveling by air a dreaded ordeal. We now have to endure long lines waiting while pretending that we aren't mentally profiling everyone else in our line. It creates an atmosphere of distrust and disgust. The stripping down and shedding of all outerwear is demanding and demeaning. As for shoes, who can remember to wear slip-ons? I never do until I find myself laboriously undoing my tie-ons in a supremely unflattering position.

Whine B: I hate having to strip.

Cure: The **"check everything"** cure is just a band-aid for getting through security. By everything I mean everything except your ID and ticket. This is the only chance you have to zip through security unscalded by suspicion and humility, and even that is not a given if you have a foreign accent, forget to take off your sunglasses or just have "one of those faces." I've thought of going through nude but I suppose that would be seen as a protest of some kind. My objective is purely convenience-oriented; besides, I wouldn't want to repulse staff or fellow travelers—or, God forbid, put the idea of a cavity search in anyone's head...

4

Lost Baggage

✈✈✈✈ ✈✈✈✈ ✈✈✈✈

The scientific theory I like best is that the rings of Saturn are composed entirely of lost airline bags.

—*Mark Russell*

Whine A: Oh, No! Not again!

Why: As soon as people find out you're an airline type person, all they want to talk about are their lost bags. It's as if they think you could do something about it or that you even care. Lost bags are the universal complaint that does not discriminate against any class of flyer. Whether you fly first class or economy (known to flight attendants as low or no class) your bags are all treated equally—without the slightest care in the world.

Whine B: But I need my clothes.

Cure: The **"carry-on bags only"** cure works for me. It is the only way of making sure that you don't end up languishing at the lost claims counter. The officials there pretend that they really care but they don't. To them, one lost bag is just like any other. If they've seen one, they've seen them all—except for *your* bag. Do not under any circumstance hassle your check-in person. To do so could mean that while you are flying to Los Angeles, your bags could be going to London. Trust me. It happens. And don't forget to pack all of your explosive perfume and toiletries in that soon-to-be-lost bag, as you are no longer allowed to carry on such dangerous and subversive items.

5
Jet Lag

✈✈✈✈ ✈✈✈✈ ✈✈✈✈

> **Airplane travel is nature's way of making you look like your passport photo.**
>
> —*Vice-President Al Gore*

Whine A: Oh, God, I look awful!

Why: Everyone knows that traveling through time zones creates a feeling of malaise and displacement we have come to call jet lag, but few of us are ready for the natural irritability it breeds or the dehydrating and depressing physical effects that always come with it. Ready or not, though, jet lag is one of those unavoidable annoyances of air travel that causes lots of whining, and no one ever seems to have any good advice about how to cure it.

Whine B: I'm never going to feel normal again.

Cure: If you can swing it, the **"extra day"** cure works best. This should be easy for leisure travelers: simply plan an extra day at each end of your trip, to consist of nothing but getting over your jet lag. Whatever comfort means to you, that's what this day is for: stay in bed watching TV, nap the afternoon away with an eye-mask on, take a long, meandering walk, fall asleep watching a foreign movie with no subtitles in a warm, dark cinema, or sit in a park people-watching until your eyes glaze over—the possibilities are endless when you have no plans. If you're a business traveler, on the other hand, willing to withstand jet lag—up to a point—for profit, power naps, moisturizers, plenty of water intake and a well-timed cocktail or two will have to do.

6
Big Crowds, Small Seats

✈✈✈✈　✈✈✈✈　✈✈✈✈

> **Elementary, my dear Watson, elementary.**
>
> —*Sherlock Holmes*

Whine A: It's so cramped!

Why: Yup, it's true: more and more people are flying, which means more and more passengers are being squeezed on more and more planes with smaller and smaller seats. It's very simple when you think about it, but that doesn't stop it from being frustrating. Only contortionists can accommodate the fold-down table nowadays; and good luck negotiating which one of you is going to get the armrest. Lack of space is also another way airlines stop us from whining about their lack of food service, since even the smallest meal will make husky and slim people alike feel too big for their cramped quarters.

Whine B: These seats are ridiculous.

Cure: The "**dress for comfort**" cure is one that many of us from earlier generations still can't get used to, having had mothers that dressed us up before boarding a plane as if we were going to meet the President; but the days of looking sharp while flying have sadly gone by the wayside along with legroom, head space and three-course meals. The only way to stay comfortable in the downscaled seats of today's jam-packed flying buses is to make sure your clothes won't bind or discomfort you in any way. Throw your vanity out the window and fly in your jammies if you dare; but at least slip into *something* more comfortable.

7
Crying Babies

✈✈✈✈ ✈✈✈✈ ✈✈✈✈

> **In America there are two classes of travel—
> first class, and with children.**
>
> —*Robert Benchley*

Whine A: Why me?

Why: It is one of the laws of airline travel that you will always be near the crying baby or the kid kicking the back of your seat. Do you think it's because the airlines know that this will bother you more than any other passenger and they're doing it just to get your goat? I do! They want everyone to have something special to complain about so that they won't turn their attentions toward the crowded plane, small seats, lack of food or surly service.

Whine B: Will it ever stop?

Cure: I advocate that you **"ask for a new seat"** right from the start. If you are serious about your peace both inner and outer, it is worth the risk of being thought of as a "child-hater." The parents will get over it, and even if they don't, who cares? They're the ones stuck with the crying brat. Your bravery will bear itself out when you see that, by the end of the flight, everyone will wish they had done the same thing. If the obnoxious kids making everyone's already trying flight all the more miserable happen to be yours, just pretend that you don't know them.

8
Turbulence

✈✈✈✈ ✈✈✈✈ ✈✈✈✈

If black boxes survive air crashes, why don't they make the whole plane out of that stuff?

—George Carlin

Whine A: I don't feel good. Here we go again.

Why: Turbulence is God's way of reminding you to say your prayers and start living the way you promised you would during the last terrifying time you thought for sure you were going down. As a former flight attendant, I can safely say that turbulence can happen out of the blue no matter how great the pilot is. The only thing that can be predicted about turbulence is that when it occurs, the coffee your friendly flight attendants rush through the aisles to serve you afterwards is bound to be less than piping hot, and the stronger the turbulence, the colder the coffee.

Whine B: We're all gonna die!

Cure: There are all sorts of great cures for turbulence besides saying your prayers. I have tried them all and my favorite one is the **"pass out"** cure. You can accomplish this most expediently by taking sleeping pills or getting drunk. I recommend the pills because they are quiet and painless. Getting drunk can be loud and obnoxious, and you run the risk of a horrid hangover to go along with your jet lag. Nobody likes a drunk, but they will admire someone who can calmly doze through chaos, commotion, or—God forbid—a freefall to a certainly painful and fiery death.

9
Flight Delays

✈✈✈✈ ✈✈✈✈ ✈✈✈✈

**Hell, which every frequent traveler knows,
is in Concourse D* of O'Hare Airport.**

—*Dave Barry*

*There is no concourse D at O'Hare.

Whine A: But I'll be late for...

Why: Delays are caused by events that are beyond anyone's control, especially the airlines'—or at least that's what they want you to think. It's either too many passengers, not enough planes or crews, unreliable mechanicals or an always-convenient natural disaster, all of which you're sure are perfectly good excuses, but that doesn't change the fact that you are going to miss whatever you're going to miss and—more enragingly—that you're bored out of your head.

Whine B: They're not telling us anything!

Cure: The **"It's better than being in prison"** cure is the only one that seems to work in this situation. When stuck in a windowless, over-crowded airport with bad food, disorienting lighting, stale air and brain-teasing acoustics, I always think about how much more panicked, bored, fatigued and restless I would feel if behind bars. Not that I have ever done anything that would even remotely come close to landing me in the slammer, but it's the only place I can think of that would be worse than being stuck in an airport on a forcefully extended layover. Putting this in perspective will allow you to go with the flow and weather your wasted time like a pro.

10
Food, or the Lack of it

✈✈✈✈ ✈✈✈✈ ✈✈✈✈

The most dangerous thing about flying is
the risk of starving to death.

—Dick Depew

Whine A: What food?

Why: Ever since all the airlines decided to declare bankruptcy, there has been little or no food service offered on most flights, at least in coach. In short, your would-be meals are now paying for upper managements' golden parachutes. This may be good news in that the average traveler no longer has to deal with the proverbial poor quality of airplane food, but as bad as they were, somehow I miss those cute little trays of beef or chicken covered in mystery sauce, with their hard-as-rock dinner rolls, overcooked veggies, and doll-sized desserts. These days, we get a "snack"...

Whine B: But I don't like peanuts.

Cure: The **"food kiosk"** cure is a new and exciting food option at all airports these days. After you get to the airport for your mandatory two to three hour early check-in and thorough security inspection, you can take your time selecting your own carry-on grub supply from any number of suppliers that provide everything from greasy fast food to fresh fruit, sandwiches and salads. You will pay prices double what you'd pay in the outside world, but since you can't bring fresh food through security, this expense falls under the category of "just desserts" for hungry and deserving travelers.

Best Overall Remedy for Whining About Flying
The Chocolate Cure

More than anything else, the sensation is one of perfect peace mingled with an excitement that strains every nerve to the utmost, if you can conceive of such a combination.

—*Wilbur Wright*

Yes, I intimately know the combination of feelings of which Mr. Wright spoke, and the only way I have ever found to meld them together into one of manageable calm is through frequent and liberal chocolate consumption. I have been using this cure to help me cope with many aspects of life for many years. To ward against my terror of flying, I have always taken a chocolate candy bar along with me on every flight. It is my security blanket. I have it with me at all times just in case the plane is going to crash. I rationalize that even if dying is terrible, at least I will die with chocolate in my mouth. Now that I am older, I have started to take two candy bars with me just in case I will need one after I've already eaten the first one—which is almost always before take off.

I have been a chocolate addict for over 50 years. It has been my passion and I have blissfully spent countless hours researching and taste testing chocolate. Because I am a woman, I can also be an expert on lots of things, chocolate included. Women have known forever that chocolate has made them feel better. Our bodies crave it. It has been doing medicinal duty ever since Eve found the first cocoa bean in the Garden of Eden, and now modern science is finally validating this fact. This is wonderful news and I intend to spread the word: Chocolate is not the problem. It is the solution.

Aside from helping with my flying fears, it has been the solution to so many other problems in my life. It has improved my blood flow, delayed the growth of gray hair and has helped me get better at Sudoko. Chocolate will even reduce violence. I used to have to continually stop myself from yelling at my husband or kicking the dog before it became one of my major food groups. In any case, my husband can't hear anymore and the dog died.

As for coming out of the chocolate closet, it didn't happen overnight. One day at a time, I really had to work the step-by-step recovery program. I had to give up trying to quit and then surrender to admitting it was a healthy habit. Once I did this, I wanted to know more about my new best friend and former addiction.

I turned to the Internet, industry experts and my own circle of close advisors for my research. From the Web, I learned that Christopher Columbus brought the first cocoa beans back to Europe. He was quoted as saying, "It is a divine drink which builds up resistance and fights fatigue." Later, Casanova, who drank it before his seductions, proved without a doubt the fatigue-resisting properties of which Columbus had spoken. I also found out that, historically, only the rich and powerful could afford the chocolate experience—and thanked my lucky stars that I was born in a time of chocolate for all.

In spite of my yearning to spread the word to one and all, I also desperately wanted to become a chocolate snob, so I used my radio show on BigMediaUSA.com to entice real experts to share their knowledge with me. I interviewed and started to hob-knob with big-wigs from Hersheys, Mars USA, Amber Lyn Chocolates and Sweetriots. I especially enjoyed meeting Tracey Downey, whose handmade Big Mouth Chocolates are named after her dad, the legendary Morten Downey, Jr.

Curtis Stone, the Australian lad starring in *The Take Home Chef* on TLC and one of *People* magazine's sexiest men of the year, visited my show praising Green & Black's Organic Chocolate; and thanks to John Scharffenberger of the famous and well-respected Scharffen Berger Chocolate Maker, I have adopted a new mantra: "Chocolate is the new broccoli." John explained to me that chocolate can be the ultimate health food, and if he's comfortable with that, I'm comfortable with that, aren't you?

As for my personal advisors, Paul, my hairdresser, is a certified M&M expert and lifelong lover of chocolate who has given me much support and input, as have my workout girlfriends at Curves—fellow chocoholics one and all. My associates from National Charity League, all of whom have raised teenage daughters, have also provided expert advice over the years.

Chocolate is not only a quick cure for whining about flying and various other maladies, but it also provides guilt-free gratification without an expiration date. Experts agree with me that it can cure anything, and it may even increase your sexual appetite: hot chocolate and Viagra are said to work wonders together. It is truly a healthy and comforting tonic for all situations—and all ages!

But like I said, it took me a long time to go from low-esteem chocolate addict to confident chocolate lover. I have gone public as an example to my grandchildren, who are just discovering the joys of chocophilia, and for everyone who is addicted to anything or anyone in the hopes that they will stop their current addiction and switch to chocolate.

Believe a reformed whiner when it comes to this indispensable cure: If you consume chocolate daily then you will be a cool, calm and collected character...even when soaring through the atmosphere in a flammable hunk of metal at 700 miles per hour.

**The desire to reach for the sky
runs deep in our human psyche.**

—*Cesar Pelli*

Chapter One

Children

Kids and whining go together like peanut butter and jelly. I have discovered that most kids can whine about anything, anytime and anywhere, as long as it will embarrass their parents. Normal children do this all the time because they are experts at never acting normal in public.

Most kids love to whine about sharing things. Every parent knows the drill. If it's something that's in my hand, then it's mine; if it's broken, then it's yours. Then there is my personal favorite between siblings: the classic and mysterious "He's looking at me" whine.

Of course, all the experts will tell you that there is only one way to raise children. Unfortunately, so far no one seems to agree what that one way actually is. I have some ideas, but I won't belabor them here. It's far more fun and profitable to sit back while enjoying the divine ultimate payback: watching my kids try to raise their own little darlings.

Top Ten
Children's Whines

🍎 🍎 🍎 🍎   🍎 🍎 🍎 🍎   🍎 🍎 🍎 🍎

#1   Going to Bed

#2   Sharing

#3   Taking Turns

#4   Waking Up for School

#5   Babysitters

#6   Taking a Bath

#7   Homework

#8   Brushing Teeth

#9   Where to Sit in the Car

#10   He's Looking at Me

It's mine...
If it looks exactly like mine.
If it's yours and I steal it.
If I *think* it's mine.

But...if it's broken, it's yours.

—*My siblings...and probably yours*

1
Going to Bed

🍎 🍎 🍎 🍎   🍎 🍎 🍎 🍎   🍎 🍎 🍎 🍎

**Anyone who thinks the art of conversation is dead
ought to tell a child to go to bed.**

—Robert Gallagher

Whine A: Do I have to?

Why: This is the number one thing that children of all ages whine about. It is their universal reason to whine, something they all do. Nobody wants the party to end, and children will usually let you know this in their most irritating, annoying, whining voice, hoping to get their way while driving you crazy. From the time they are toddlers, they know that bedtime is the worst time of the day for them. Likewise, they know it is the best time for parents, which makes it even more tempting for them to whine, thus besmirching any quietude said parents may carve out for themselves. Unfortunately, it is simply not in children's nature to want to sleep. It is only when they become teenagers that they crave sleep, and then only in the mornings.

Whine B: Can't I stay up a little longer?

Cure: I have had a lot of luck with the **"Because I said so!"** cure when accompanied by the "look" that only a loving mother can give when she is exhausted. The best way to stop the whining, though, is to make a game of bedtime with songs, stories and lots of love. A visit from the tickle bug is fun for them and you too, even if they do think they're "too old for it." Remember to comfort them with a small night-light and their favorite stuffed animals—and don't forget the binkie!

2
Sharing

🍎 🍎 🍎 🍎   🍎 🍎 🍎 🍎   🍎 🍎 🍎 🍎

> **There is only one way to raise kids.**
> **Unfortunately, no one knows what it is.**
>
> —*January Jones*

Whine A: Do I have to?

Why: Sharing is one of the hardest lessons that you will ever teach your children. It is not in their nature to want to divide things up with others. By nature, they are all little hoarders who are learning how to be territorial. It is part of their self-preservation instinct not to share. It is especially hard to share their toys, favorite stuffed animals, best pals or parents with each other, especially if the other party is also having a hard time with it, which is always the case by definition. Face it: Children just don't like other people to have what they have—and this unfortunately seems to be the way with most adults these days as well!

Whine B: I don't want to.

Cure: The **"sharing is fun"** cure is an effective concept, but if you can't con them into it, better switch to the **"Because I said so!"** cure, which is one of my all time favorites. Remember, it is all in the eyes and tone. You must perfect your "look" so they know you mean business, and an effective and believable tone comes only with years of practice. Do praise your child when they divide things up with others. It makes them feel good about themselves, and it is, after all, what all the big kids do. Well, at least some of them do it.

3
Taking Turns

🍎 🍎 🍎 🍎 🍎 🍎 🍎 🍎 🍎 🍎 🍎 🍎

You can learn many things from children.
How much patience you have, for instance.

—Franklin P. Jones

Whine A: *It's my turn now.*

Why: Taking turns is a hard lesson for any child to learn, and especially for an only child. Somehow you must convince them that taking turns is fun. If you fail, they will have no friends or playmates besides their parents and grandparents. As they grow older, they will master the art of taking turns quickly with their little friends but not so quickly with their siblings. Waiting is difficult for anyone under five years of age—or even under 50. The hardest part of taking turns is being second, or third, or.... It's just not as much fun as going first.

Whine B: *It's **never** my turn.*

Cure: I had a lot of luck with the **"time out or go to bed instead"** cure when my children refused to share. Needless to say, they excelled at sharing with friends and sometimes even on rare occasions with their siblings. It helps to remind the younger ones that it is what the big kids do. Teaching them how to wait their turn with grace and patience early in life will prepare them for all the waiting in lines they will encounter as they grow up and grow old in such hallowed halls of patience-testing as the DMV, the supermarket and the post office.

4
Waking Up for School

🍎 🍎 🍎 🍎   🍎 🍎 🍎 🍎   🍎 🍎 🍎 🍎

> **What is a home without children?**
> **Quiet!**
>
> —*Henny Youngman*

Whine A: Go away! Let me sleep.

Why: Most children hate to get up once they start school. Prior to beginning school, they may have loved waking up before dawn and making sure everyone else was up, too, but things have changed. Face it, no matter what your age, waking up can be a drag, and it is especially difficult on those cold, rainy dark days of winter. For children, however, I have found that inclement weather prevents rising only on school days. On weekends, they are up early even if it's raining or snowing outside, searching for sugar-coated cereal and watching cartoons by dawn's early light.

Whine B: I can't wake up! I'm too tired.

Cure: My favorite morning wake-up cure was to sing the **"Wakey, wakey, eggs and bakey"** song to my children, which would make them get up just to make me stop singing. This song is an extremely effective cure for wake-up whining, especially if you have an irritating voice like most mothers do, at least to their children. Another great cure is to buy them their own alarm clock once they start learning how to tell time. Make them responsible for setting it and turning it off in the morning—just like Mommy and Daddy do. Hint: Place said alarm clock far away from your child's bed so as to stall his or her learning curve with the snooze button.

5
Babysitters

🍎 🍎 🍎 🍎   🍎 🍎 🍎 🍎   🍎 🍎 🍎 🍎

A child is a curly dimpled lunatic.

—*Ralph Waldo Emerson*

Whine A: I don't like her.

Why: This is your child's opportunity to use a surefire, no-miss weapon on you: the guilt factor. It may not be a fair tactic but it is effective. It is especially successful with first-time parents who are just learning the ropes when it comes to the whims and wiles of their children. All children intuitively know that it is very hard for a parent to walk out the door when those sweet little eyes are filled with tears.

Whine B: Don't leave me! I'll miss you.

Cure: I am not a big fan of the **"bribery"** cure since I know it can come back and bite you when you least expect it, but it's the easiest way to get out the door sometimes. I prefer to call it by the far less incriminating title of the **"promise them a surprise"** cure. In fact, bribery, whether blatant or not, will get you through most whining encounters with your offspring. Sure, there are other cures that can be used to battle back against their guilt attacks, but like it or not, bribery works best. Another way to deal with the babysitter whine that may not always be convenient is to use sitters that your children adore. Grandparents would fit into this category. Despite how much they love you, it is always a treat for all of them to have you out of the way.

6
Taking a Bath

🍎 🍎 🍎 🍎 🍎 🍎 🍎 🍎 🍎 🍎 🍎 🍎

- **Boy (n): a noise with dirt on it.**
- **Girl (n): sugar and spice and everything nice, especially when taking a bubble bath.**

—Not Your Average Dictionary

Whine A: Do I have to?

Why: Little boys and most grown men hate taking baths. There is something in their DNA that keeps them from wanting to soak in water unless it is a swimming pool, the ocean or a mud puddle. They love playing in dirt and adore smelling like little pigs. This whine made it to the top ten because for every little girl who adores taking a bubble bath, there are ten little boys who would rather drink molten lava than spend any considerable amount of time in the tub.

Whine B: I did already...yesterday.

Cure: First and foremost, you must establish that this is not a topic for debate. This is a hard concept to convey to any boy or tomboy. It is best to relax and wait until you can teach them the "**take a shower**" cure. Once they are old enough to shower by themselves you will never be able to get them out. Some men even shave, plan their schedules or use their cell phones in the shower. It can become a safe, soggy haven from their mothers, wives, kids and anyone else they want to avoid.

7

Homework

🍎 🍎 🍎 🍎   🍎 🍎 🍎 🍎   🍎 🍎 🍎 🍎

Life is simple. It's just not easy.

—Susan Vopicka

Whine A: Do I have to?

Why: For some reason, most little girls love to do homework and most boys hate it passionately; however, this dynamic changes for girls when they get older and more interested in boys than their homework. I think the reason that some little boys hate homework is because all they want to do is to play, all day and all night. It is a part of their DNA that continues to unfold throughout their lives. For that matter, can you think of any man, woman or child who would rather work than play?

Whine B: I'll do it later.

Cure: The homework battle is one of the toughest ones you will ever fight with your kids. I have fought this good fight through two generations, and have found only one surefire remedy: the **"threat with consequences"** cure. For example, you might say, "Unless you do your homework right now, you will have to (fill in something that they really hate doing)." This can be an ugly and confrontational technique, but it usually makes them see the error of their ways, and makes it easier for them to do what they don't really want to do. The difficult part will be when your children try to explain it to their shrinks twenty years from now.

8
Brushing Teeth

🍎 🍎 🍎 🍎 🍎 🍎 🍎 🍎 🍎 🍎 🍎 🍎

A characteristic of a normal child is they don't act normal very often—especially about their teeth.

—Kelly Jonassen

Whine A: Do I have to?

Why: Brushing teeth takes time away from the fun things that kids would rather be doing; plus they know that brushing their teeth at night is a definite move in the direction of going to bed. It is a ritual they all try to avoid, as with all things leading up to bedtime. As for brushing their teeth after they eat, don't be ridiculous. None of them will do this unless you make them do it by brute force. This is not a cure that I advocate due to child abuse laws.

Whine B: I already did.

Cure: I always had good luck with telling my children that if they didn't brush their teeth, they would have to do the **"Mr. Cavity"** cure. That meant a visit to the dentist. Now, this was something they could *really* whine about. Actually, do you know anyone either child or adult who doesn't at least want to whine about going to the dentist? It's simply a fact of life that going to the dentist is no fun—even for dentists, I've been told, though they do seem to be content—if not in fact enjoying themselves—when they are the ones holding the drills.

9
Where to Sit in the Car

🍎 🍎 🍎 🍎　🍎 🍎 🍎 🍎　🍎 🍎 🍎 🍎

> **A child can create situations**
> **that no mother can fix.**
>
> —*January Jones*

Whine A: I call front seat.

Why: Every child wants to sit up front in the carpool. At first I thought it was to be near me, but then I realized that it was all about music control. The child up front has immediate access to the car radio, which bestows upon that child a certain power over everyone in the car, including the driver. This is a great opportunity for children to traumatize others, and to constantly war about their ever-changing pecking order. Unfortunately, age and size discrimination are carpool realities. The oldest and biggest were usually my front seat companions. You must remember that sitting next to the chief in tribal life is a big deal!

Whine B: He took my place.

Cure: When the kids started driving me crazy with their bickering in the car, I would use the "**ultimate ultimatum**" cure on them. This involved them being forced to listen to my music on the radio—and in extreme cases, even my singing—until they all sat still and shut up. Due to their extreme and ingrained dislike for anything I liked, mostly because it simply wasn't cool, this was one of my cleverest and quickest cures. I adore sharing it with parents who I see carpooling children on the highways and by-ways of life.

10

He's looking at me.

🍎 🍎 🍎 🍎　🍎 🍎 🍎 🍎　🍎 🍎 🍎 🍎

A child can ask questions
that a wise mother cannot answer.

—Lisa Moellering

Whine A: Tell him to stop it.

Why: An older child tormenting a younger one always causes this whine. It is a ritual that has been practiced by siblings since Cain and Abel squared off against one another in the Garden of Eden. This scenario usually starts with the youngest child whining that they are being "looked at." Next, the older child will deny that they are looking at anyone, least of all the despised younger child... and so the cycle begins.

Whine B: He's still doing it.

Cure: When this mysterious and chronic situation arose during my kids' early childhoods, I usually tried to explain to them that there was no law against looking at someone. It never worked but it made sense to me, and I spent countless hours vainly trying to convince them of the same. I tried to look wise when using this technique, but my children always found a weak point in my logic, eventually driving me crazy. As a last resort, I would make them all do the **"put on your sunglasses"** cure, whether inside or out, sunny or not. That way no one could look at anyone or see anyone looking at them, and it certainly made me laugh seeing them sitting around our TV room silently watching cartoons through their shades, careful to not even glance at one another.

Best Overall Remedy for Whining Children

The Norwegian Ris-paa-rumpen Cure

This valuable method for curbing whining in children was brought to this country by my husband's Norwegian parents. We called them BaBa and MorMor. They were wise and wonderful, and dearly loved by their entire family, especially their grandchildren. When any of them began whining about anything, asking the child a simple question initiated the cure: "Do you want a Ris-paa-rumpen?" It is not so much the question as it is the manner in which it is asked that makes it such an effective method.

You may ask, "What is a Ris-paa-rumpen?" As far as I can explain, it is our Norwegian family's word for a little love pat that is applied gently and lovingly to a child's bottom. What makes this cure so amazingly effective is that every parent or grandparent can style their own delivery for maximum effect. My husband would take the child quite firmly by the arm and stare straight into their eyes when asking them if they really wanted a Ris-paa-rumpen.

Truthfully, I have never heard a child respond with a "yes" to this question. And in case you may want to report us to the child protective services, the actual Ris-paa-rumpen cure has never had to be used in our family that I can remember! As for our children, don't believe a thing they say as their memories are not to be trusted after so many years.

Chapter Two

Teenagers

From my own experience as a teenager and then raising four, I can honestly say that teenagers and whining go together like curfews and cars. The reality is that before you have babies, nobody ever tells you the truth about teenagers. If anyone did, then it would probably be the end of civilization as we know it.

I've noticed that teens are always whining about having nothing to do, yet they are always too busy if you need them to do something for you. Also, they love to whine about ephemeral matters that all parents know are only part of the growing pains that all teenagers go through. But just try explaining this to your growing teenager.

Watching your own children go through the sometimes tragic trials and tribulations of a normal adolescence is like living through a bad case of the flu. It's horrible, but you have to remember that even though there's no cure, eventually it will get better and go away. And then they will go away...and find new things to whine about. Therefore, it's always good to keep in mind that a whining teenager at home is easier to handle and heal than a whining adult child adrift in the world. Now try not to worry. Even if time doesn't stand still, you still may have time.

> **You know your children are becoming teenagers when they stop asking where they came from and start refusing to tell you where they're going.**
>
> —*January Jones*

Top Ten
Teenagers' Whines

☎ ☎ ☎ ☎   ☎ ☎ ☎ ☎   ☎ ☎ ☎ ☎

#1   TV and Computers

#2   Homework and Grades

#3   Money

#4   Curfew

#5   Driving

#6   Dating

#7   Popularity

#8   Weight

#9   Zits and Blemishes

#10   Peer Pressure

Adolescence: *A stage between infancy and adultery.*

—*Ambrose Bierce*

1

TV and Computers

☎☎☎☎ ☎☎☎☎ ☎☎☎☎

> It is hard to decide whether growing pains are
> something teenagers have, or are.
>
> —*January Jones*

Whine A: I can't stop now.

Why: Most teenagers today are addicted to television and their computers. They are well-versed and fluent in this technology since they've used it from their earliest years. It is as familiar and comforting for them to watch TV or be on their computer as it might be for their grandparents to take a nap or a relaxing walk. TV and computers are escapes from a world teenagers aren't quite ready to join. You can't blame them. The world is a pretty scary place right now for all of us.

Whine B: Why are you bothering me?

Cure: It is indeed a challenge to control or limit a teenager's addiction to television or their computers. If you try, they will bombard you with all sorts of whining tactics to get their way. I think the best solution would be the **"trade off"** cure. If their grades are good and their behavior even better, no problem. They can watch TV or go online whenever they want to, as long as they don't visit adult-only Websites. If grades fall, all you need to do is pull the plugs until they get better. Good luck, and believe me, you'll need it.

2
Homework and Grades

☎ ☎ ☎ ☎　☎ ☎ ☎ ☎　☎ ☎ ☎ ☎

> **It is hard to convince a high school student that he will encounter a lot of problems more difficult than those of algebra and geometry.**
>
> —*Edgar W. Howe*

Whine A: Stop bugging me.

Why: The "homework is hard and horrible" whine has been going on ever since the first high school welcomed its first freshman class. Nobody likes doing it unless they are "weird" or something, your "normal" teenager will tell you. Teenagers love whining about homework, especially with all of their friends, who, of course, don't like to do it either. It is their way of bonding by uniting against their common enemies: their teachers, who assign it, and their parents, who quite unreasonably expect them to do it.

Whine B: It's no big deal.

Cure: Try to make the best of a bad situation. Keep in mind that this too will pass when they finally come into their own, usually around the time they discover a subject or teacher that they adore. Until then, I recommend the **"car keys"** cure as an incentive for teenagers with driver's licenses to do their homework. With younger teens, grounding them is your only choice. Unfortunately, this can sometimes be a bigger punishment for you than for them. I know this is hard but you can't give up. It helps to impress upon them what hideous employment opportunities await those who fail to do their homework and get good grades.

3
Money

☎☎☎☎ ☎☎☎☎ ☎☎☎☎

**If you want to recapture your youth,
just cut off his allowance.**

—Al Bernstein

Whine A: I'm broke.

Why: It is exceedingly difficult to teach teenagers the value of money in this world. Nobody has enough and everybody needs more. Materialism rules our global culture and creates ridiculous desires and longings in our young people. Having money can create a sense of entitlement that is often followed by disappointment, and not having it...well, everyone knows how fun not having money is. Whining happens when teenagers expect more and then get less from their parents.

Whine B: Everybody has more than me.

Cure: The best remedy for teenagers who whine about money is the **"get a job"** cure. Some would consider this cruel and unusual punishment. Those parties would most likely be your kids and their friends. All others questioned or involved will most likely agree with you that this is an essential backbone building experience for every budding adult. If things get unpleasant after the work suggestion, you could always consider asking them to start paying you rent. This will both insult them and remind them that your rules are law under your roof—a good rejoinder when faced with any sort of teen rebellion, in fact!

4
Curfew

☎☎☎☎ ☎☎☎☎ ☎☎☎☎

**Teenagers complain there's nothing to do,
then stay out all night doing it.**

—Bob Phillips

Whine A: Why can't I stay out longer?

Why: Although curfews are necessary for teens, they are very tricky to enforce. The old saying that some things are easier said than done definitely applies to setting and maintaining curfews for adventuresome, quickly maturing teens. You will be up against all the forces of nature trying to get your kids home at a decent hour. It behooves you to do so as soon and as often as possible, though, or you may end up spending most of your life exhausted from waiting up for them to get home.

Whine B: Everyone else can.

Cure: I was very diligent about tracking the trails of my first two daughters, but by the time the third one got old enough to go out on her own, I was too tired to do much tracking. Keeping track of teenagers on the loose has always been a frustratingly unmasterable art to worried mothers and fathers everywhere; however, with the advent of cellular technology comes the paradigm-shifting "**cell phone**" cure, which allows parents to at least have a fighting chance of keeping track of their wayward teens. To cure teens who never answer when you call or call when you ask, remind them that you can always get them a phone with GPS capabilities that will chart their every move—that should shock and insult them into keeping in touch.

5
Driving

☎ ☎ ☎☎   ☎ ☎☎ ☎   ☎ ☎☎ ☎

**Never lend your car to anyone
to whom you have given birth.**

—Erma Bombeck

Whine A: When can I start driving?

Why: Driving is a rite of passage for teenagers and an excellent reason for their parents to increase their insurance coverage. It is also a golden opportunity for whining, with all sorts of possibilities for dramatic subterfuge. It is your teenager's big chance for freedom from you, and they will fight for it with all they've got. All they want to do is escape with their friends and get away from their parents by hitting the road. When this war is waged, expect to come out the loser. You will end up with gray hair and frazzled nerves to go with your extremely high liability insurance rates.

Whine B: What's wrong with now?

Cure: I lean towards the **"let their fathers teach them how to drive"** cure for this one. Some things are better handled by fathers and when it comes to teaching driving, Dads seem to do it better. This is especially true for girls. My third and final daughter hit three cars in one day, two of which were her sisters' vehicles. Boys seem to catch on faster, or at least they like to make you think they do. Once they have learned the finer points of driving to your satisfaction and they're safely on the road, you will worry about them anyway. At this time, you will need to make an appointment with your hairdresser to handle all your new gray hairs.

6
Dating

☎ ☎ ☎ ☎   ☎ ☎ ☎ ☎   ☎ ☎ ☎ ☎

The best substitute for experience is being sixteen.

—Raymond Duncan

Whine A: When will I be old enough?

Why: All of your worst nightmares will come true when your teenagers start to date, and they will always want to start dating sooner than you think they should. They will sit by the phone for hours waiting for their true love of the moment to call, and this is just the beginning of a cycle of manic feelings that will be quickly followed by a visit to Heartbreak Hotel. Everyone knows true love is hard to find, but teenagers seem to like to try over and over again as quickly as possible, which creates plenty of situations for very potent whining indeed.

Whine B: What's wrong with now?

Cure: I favored **"the love them and leave them"** cure for my children. Basically it went like this: If things were good with the new love of their life then I loved them too. If things weren't working out, I usually advocated leaving them in the ocean to drown. Truth be told, I never liked any of my children's potential suitors when they were teenagers, but then, what parent ever thinks anyone is good enough or pure enough to win the hearts of their physically grown, but still very young and inexperienced, darlings?

7
Popularity

☎ ☎ ☎ ☎   ☎ ☎ ☎ ☎   ☎ ☎ ☎ ☎

As a teenager you are at the last stage in your life when you will be happy to hear that the phone is for you.

—*Fran Lebowitz*

Whine A: Nobody likes me.

Why: Whining about a lack of popularity is so common with teenagers as to seem a completely normal and viable way of expressing themselves. It is because they are at the most sensitive, delicate time of their emotional development that fitting in becomes an issue. Any form of rejection is devastating to them, especially if it comes from the opposite sex. Of course, they'll whine about not being in the "in" group at school until they see that the "in" group was never as "in" as they thought they were—and then they'll whine about that.

Whine B: I don't have any friends.

Cure: It is about as easy to teach teenagers how to be popular as it is to impress upon them that the popularity they do gain in high school will mean absolutely nothing once they graduate. I tried to remind my teenagers that **"the smile cure"** worked wonders for me many years ago while trying to gain a footing in my own high school pecking order. I smiled at everyone, and guess what happened—they started smiling back. I even smiled at people who didn't know me just to see them wonder who I was or how I knew them. Smiling is a contagious disease that most people are more than happy to catch, popular or not.

8
Weight

☎ ☎ ☎☎   ☎ ☎ ☎☎   ☎ ☎ ☎☎

> **My adolescence progressed normally:**
> **Enough misery to keep the death wish my usual state.**
>
> —*Faye Moskowitz*

Whine A: I'm so fat.

Why: Weight is a real whining issue for many teenage girls and some boys too. Nobody likes being fat or wants others to notice that they have a weight problem. It's not fun and it's a valid reason for a little whining in my opinion, but let's not go overboard. I agree that it's not fair that some people can eat like pigs and never gain an ounce while the rest of us gain weight just by looking at food. It certainly sucks!

Whine B: I can't lose weight.

Cure: There are so many cures for weight loss that I don't know where to begin. My favorite is the "**I love you just the way you are**" cure, the repetition of which will go a long way toward boosting your teens' self-esteem even if they don't seem to respond at first. For teens who can't stop complaining despite doing nothing about their weight problems, encourage emulation of someone whom they admire both physically and spiritually. Perhaps they may even focus on reaching the standard of perfection they see in this idol. Rest assured, it won't be you.

9
Zits and Other Blemishes

☎☎☎☎ ☎☎☎☎ ☎☎☎☎

At fourteen you don't need sickness or death for tragedy.

—*Jessamyn West*

Whine A: It's not fair.

Why: Everything changes for children after the first twelve years are over. Hormonally speaking, it will not be an easy time for your teenagers. Emotionally speaking, it will be an even worse time for you as their parent. Their highs and lows will leave them, and you, in despair, and nothing seems to cause more highs and lows in teenagers than the relative state of their skin. God forbid one of my daughter's would break out before a date, as darkness would befall the entire household for days.

Whine B: I'm so ugly, and it's all your fault.

Cure: Accept the fact that nothing you say or do will make things okay for your teenagers while they have zits. It's your fault and no one else's. I recommend finding a good skin doctor who can help. Also, the **"facials are wonderful"** cure can aid not only their complexion but also their self esteem. Good luck, and remember any fees you pay to a doctor or aesthetician will be money well spent when you see them smiling again. If you're lucky, maybe they'll even smile at you, but don't count on it.

10
Peer Pressure

☎☎☎☎   ☎☎☎☎   ☎☎☎☎

> The young have the same problem,
> how to rebel and conform at the same time.
> They have now solved this by defying their parents
> and copying one another.
>
> —*Quentin Crisp*

Whine A: Everybody does it.

Why: The only thing that matters to teenagers at this time in their lives are their friends and what their friends say and do. The whining starts when things don't go well for them with their friends. What their friends think about them is crucial to their existence, and if what these friends think is negative, your teenager's fragile world will come tumbling down; therefore, your teen will do everything he can not to rock the boat. Peer pressure must be handled with care. If you trash their friends, they will trash you.

Whine B: Why can't I? It's not fair.

Cure: The best advice is to try to steer your teens towards **"the nice friends"** cure. If you start early enough exposing them to the kind of peers who have the qualities and habits you'd like to see in your own child, it might work. The good news is that someday in the future, you may even become one of their friends. Try to be patient while waiting for that to happen, and remember that my cure is easier than locking them up and throwing away the key—and safer than locking them out.

Best Overall Remedy for Whining Teenagers

The Time Out or You're Grounded Cure

This is a theory as old as the invention of clocks. Most people are familiar with the time-out process, which is traditionally used mostly for young children. Basically, it involves a time of silence and solitary reflection for whining children until they can pull themselves together and re-join their parents or peers.

I personally never used it with my children when they were young. As I've already mentioned, my children seldom whined, having been exposed to the Norwegian Ris-pa-rumpin Cure. When they became teenagers, though, I used it constantly, adjusting its title to the "You Are Grounded!" cure. I once grounded my out-all-night daughter for thirty years.

Both she and I can happily report to you that thirty years goes by rather quickly.

Years later, this same daughter uses the time-out cure quite effectively with her twins. The amount of time spent in the time-out starts with an amount of minutes equaling their age on the first infraction, and goes up one minute for every subsequent instance of undue whining. I can't wait to see how she calculates her grounding schedule once time marches on and they get a little older.

> **You don't have to be a poet to suffer.**
> **Adolescence is enough suffering for anyone.**
>
> —*John Ciardi*

Chapter Three

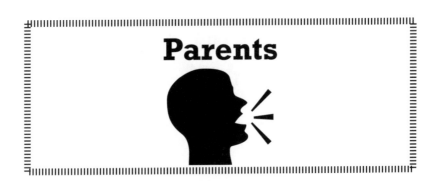

Parents

Anyone can give birth to a child, but to be a parent you must go quite a bit further than just reproducing. Isn't it interesting that humans are the only species that actually breeds on purpose? We aren't even as smart as guppies. At least they know enough to eat their kids. Instead, we allow them to devour us.

Parents and whining go together like babies and binkies. Or was that blankies? No matter, once you sign up for the Parenthood Plan there is no time off or cancellation clauses. It's a full-time job with no leave of absence unless you are good at faking amnesia or Alzheimer's.

But what else would you rather have done with your life? You would have had more money, definitely more time and certainly more privacy; however, you would have missed out on some of the most potent whining opportunities known to mankind.

You want whining? Give me a parent and I'll show you some real whiners. I know I'm supposed to say parenthood is one of the greatest institutions known to man. However, I can't say it because my husband will have me committed if I do.

If I had my child to raise all over again,
I'd build self-esteem first, and the house later.
I'd finger-paint more, and point the finger less.
I would do less correcting and more connecting.

I'd take more hikes and fly more kites.
I'd stop playing serious, and seriously play.
I'd do more hugging and less tugging.

—*Diane Loomans*

Top Ten
Parents' Whines

#1 **Money**

#2 **Children at Home**

#3 **Children Away from Home**

#4 **Jobs**

#5 **Fighting**

#6 **Discipline**

#7 **Whining**

#8 **Teenagers' Driving**

#9 **Kids' Friends**

#10 **Vacations**

Parenthood: that state of being better chaperoned
than you were before marriage.

—*Marcelene Cox*

1
Money

> Mother Nature, in her infinite wisdom, has instilled within each of us a powerful biological instinct to reproduce; this is her way of assuring that the human race, come what may, will have never have any disposable income.
>
> —*Dave Barry*

Whine A: I need more! I'm broke.

Why: Parents whine about money because there never seems to be enough. Just when you think you are getting ahead, something always happens to flatten that little cushion you've spent so much time and care fluffing up. Anything unexpected such as an illness, accident, unscheduled repair or even the wife going off the deep end at the 24-hour midnight sale at the mall can trigger a financial emergency, so whining about money is always a danger while parenting.

Whine B: Where did it go?

Cure: I suggest you consider going for the **"big insurance policy"** cure so that when you die your kids can pay off your debts and throw a big party in your honor. Or better yet, the entire family can go on a memorial cruise to celebrate your life. On second thought, why wait? Call the travel agent today...but first find a credit card that hasn't been maxed out.

2
Children at Home

> **Human are the only animals that have children on purpose—with the exception of guppies, who like to eat theirs.**
>
> —*P. J. O'Rourke*

Whine A: I can't do anything with them.

Why: Parents have been whining about their children since Adam and Eve had their problems with their boys in the Garden of Eden. The children become the center of their parent's world just by being there. They start out as such sweet, helpless babies that parents tend to fret and worry about their children long after they are no longer children, no longer helpless, and very often, no longer sweet. It's a parental prerogative that can't be changed, helped or stopped.

Whine B: They're driving me crazy.

Cure: The best cure and the hardest cure is the **"let go"** cure. Let them do their own thing. For some parents, disengaging is impossible, and sadly, they never let go, irreparably damaging both the parent-child relationship and its two participants. This is a control issue plain and simple, and one you must get over as a loving parent, despite the fact that you only want what you think is best for them and they only want what *they* think is best for themselves. That's the war, and you have to pick your battles if you're to come out victorious. If you must whine about your children, only do it with other parents. No one else will understand or care.

3
Children Away from Home

> **Your children tell you casually years later**
> **what would have killed you with worry**
> **to know at the time.**
>
> —*Mignon McLaughlin*

Whine A: I wonder if they're okay.

Why: All parents fret and worry about their children when they're not around, no matter how safely tucked into a trustworthy caretaker's pockets they may be, and especially if their whereabouts are questionable or unknown. No matter how mature and responsible your children are, and no matter how sure you are they will return at the time agreed upon without a scratch, you may still remain unable to stop worrying about them. This phenomenon has no connection whatsoever to their age since it is an ageless concern of all parents everywhere. But you *can* stop whining about it.

Whine B: I can't sleep worrying about them.

Cure: My advice in this instance is to use the "**pretend you aren't that worried, then take a sleeping pill**" cure. Showing your worry when it's unnecessary will only make your children uncomfortable, and waiting up for them is simply not an option. How will you know if they made it home safely? If you're like most parents, even a sleeping pill will not keep you from waking up when the front door ever so stealthily opens and closes in the wee hours of the morning.

4
Jobs

> **You have a lifetime to work.**
> **But children are young only once.**
>
> —*Jennie Gryzlak*

Whine A: I don't have enough time.

Why: In today's economy, with most families needing two incomes in order to survive, whining about jobs is a fact of family life. The cost of living and providing for a young family is astronomical, and it only gets more so as the family matures and develops. Whining about work is almost valid since the time you spend working is time that you could be spending with your children. Unfortunately, whining about it won't give you any more of the quality time you so desire.

Whine B: Someone *has to earn the money.*

Cure: The **"savor the moment"** cure is the most practical one here. Since you can't quit your job to be with your kids, you might as well enjoy what you're doing when you're doing it. Remember, it's about the quality of the time spent together versus the quantity, so a little can go a long way if you work it right. When you are with your children, give them 100%, your very best, all the time, no matter how limited it may be. If you are both determined and lucky, they may even repay you by giving you maybe 50 to 60 % of their best on a good day.

5
Fighting

> **When my kids become wild and unruly,**
> **I use a nice, safe playpen.**
> **When they're finished, I climb out.**
>
> —*Erma Bombeck*

Whine A: Stop it! I mean right now!

Why: Parents eventually realize that their children fighting with other small members of the family is a fact of life. It is something they all do with great delight and zeal, whether it is the older one teasing the younger or the younger one annoying the older, or any combination possible given the size and scope of your family. It is the nature of the beasts that children are, and the law of the domestic jungle in which they romp and roar, and if you want to keep a handle on it, remember that whining about it only makes you seem like you want to join in rather than referee.

Whine B: Do you want me to settle this?

Cure: The best tool that I have ever utilized to handle fighting between my children is the **"join in the fun"** cure. This works due to the fact that all children will immediately stop doing something if their parents decide they'd like to do it too. Just watch: When you ask them if they want you to join in the fray, they will always end the fight right away. There's no way on earth they want to fight with you, or see you having fun. It's much easier for children to just stop whatever they're doing rather than risk the boredom of doing it with their parents.

6
Discipline

No matter how calmly you try to referee,
parenting will eventually produce bizarre behavior,
and I'm not talking about the kids.

—*Bill Cosby*

Whine A: Do it now, or else!

Why: Disciplining children is one the hardest things that you will ever do as a parent. There is always the dilemma of doing too much or, more often, doing too little, and it's difficult finding that happy medium that is just right for your child. This is a quandary that will take all the wisdom you possess and all the endurance you can muster—along with plenty of wit. Your kids will test you every chance they get. To them, it is a matter of survival of the fittest. If they sense your weakness during a stand-off, they're prone to revert to jungle warfare, subverting your dominion over them until the next challenge. Raising your kids is the ultimate reality show.

Whine B: Did you hear what I said?!

Cure: The **"do what I say just because I say so, or else, and don't ask questions"** cure is very effective if your child knows that you mean business. This is not the time to bluff. You have to be the one in control. In fact, children do not want to be the ones in control because it is too scary, but they will never let you see that fear. They actually need you to step up to the plate and be a real parent instead of someone they might be able to get the better of without much problem.

7
Whining

> Oh wouldn't the world seem dull and flat
> with nothing whatever to grumble at?
>
> —*W.S. Gilbert*

Whine A: *All their whining is driving me crazy.*

Why: Parents whining about their kid's whining is their pathetic attempt to get other people to feel sorry for them. It doesn't work because no one in their right mind will ever feel sorry for people who have been breeding whiners. It's like a highly contagious disease that they are spreading around without any regards for others. Despite your best efforts, children will always do what you do or don't do rather than what you tell them to do or not to do. And if you whine, then whining is what the little monkeys will do, too.

Whine B: *Could you just whine a little louder?*

Cure: The **"Wait a minute, I sound as bad as they do"** cure is an effective charm when you find yourself whining about your children's whining, especially since children tend to mimic their parents rather than the other way around. Remember, they're whining because you are, most likely, and if you stop, they are much more likely to follow suit. My husband used to love trying to out whine the whiner. It was his version of "anything you can do, I can do better." It was not a very mature approach, but it made him feel better. It drove our kids so crazy that they would stop whining whenever Dad used this rather underhanded technique.

8
Teenagers' Driving

> **The child supplies the power
> but the parents have to do the steering.**
>
> —*Dr. Spock*

Whine A: Sixteen is just too young.

Why: Parents whine about their teenager's driving because it is the ultimate payback lesson. Suddenly, they are forced to remember what kind of drivers they used to be. The whining is reinforced as their teenager pulls out of the driveway headed to do exactly the same things that they did when they were teenagers. History does repeat itself, and unfortunately for most of us, this is an entirely valid whine.

Whine B: I don't know where they are anymore.

Cure: New technology has changed the playing field and it's finally starting to even things out. Nowadays, if you are a parent and don't put a GPS tracking device in your kid's car, you deserve whatever they dish out. You can actually track their every move and have a print-out ready to go over when they come home. Believe me, this is so much better than the old lie detector test that my generation of parents used to wish were available for pop interrogation sessions. Now don't go and start whining about the cost of a GPS on top of your other whining: it's expensive, but essential to an Information Age parent's sanity and survival.

9
Kids' Friends

> **Heredity is what sets parents and their children to wondering about each other.**
>
> —*Laurence J. Peter*

Whine A: Why do you like them?

Why: When you're a parent, your kids' friends will give you hundreds of things to really whine about. It's always one thing or another. You can whine about the way they dress, the things they say, the way they act, the places they hang out, the other questionable people they hang out with besides your precious child, or any other thing they do to annoy you. How do they know what really gets to you? It's simple and universal: If you like someone, then you can be sure that your kid won't like them, and vice versa.

Whine B: Can't you hang with someone better?

Cure: The only way to cure the whining urge regarding your kid's friends is to **"have your mouth taped shut or take a vow of silence."** Never, ever, and I repeat, *never*, say anything nice about someone with whom you'd like to see your kid make friends or something bad about someone you'd rather they didn't hang out with. Either way, this is worse than the Kiss of Death, for it is the dreaded Kiss of the Parent. The only thing worse than that is the Kiss of the Sibling.

10
Peer Pressure

> **A child needs your presence
> more than your presents.**
>
> —*Jesse Jackson*

Whine A: If they jumped off a bridge, would you jump too?

Why: It drives most parents crazy when they realize that the only thing their kids care about is what other kids think about them. Whining about the peer pressure their children seem absolutely driven to give into is common for parents because it's another universal complaint that's predicated on the most basic of instincts: Wild animals and kids feel safe only when they are with the herd. This can also turn into an expensive whine since your child will always want what "everyone else" has. Now if you could only figure out why "everyone else's" parents always seem to have way more money than you do...

Whine B: Why do you have to be like everyone else?

Cure: What a silly question. The answer is absolutely and very simply because they must. They can't risk being different. It is essential to let your child experience the "**copy-cat syndrome**" cure of peer pressure in order to establish their own identity. This is a ritual they all go through and somehow survive despite your efforts to stop it, so remember: just like binkies and thumb-sucking, this clone mentality that seems to have eaten their personalities, too, shall pass.

Best Overall Remedy
for Whining Parents

The Hybrid Cure

Nothing that my husband and I have ever done as parents has impressed our four children more than when we unknowingly became environmentally correct by embracing The Hybrid Cure for parental whining. When we became hybrid car owners, our parental approval ratings went through the roof. Our kids could not believe that we were bona fide members in good standing with the liberal, environmental Hollywood crowd. They were stunned and shocked that their parents were capable of joining such a hip and ecologically progressive market sector.

To tell the truth, my husband and I suffer from Obsessive Compulsive Buyers syndrome, known as OCB. We like to be the first ones on our block with anything new, especially cars. Our kids call us the Instant Gratification Generation. When they were younger, we bought one of the first Miatas off the assembly line—a stupid, impulsive purchase since the tiny convertible had barely enough room for our fat butts, no room for luggage and certainly no accommodations ample enough for my gargantuan purse. It was horribly uncomfortable.

Through our OCB, we stumbled upon the Hybrid Cure, which has been much more beneficial than that old Miata ever was. It has almost helped us to stop whining about the price of gas, and now we can drive in the carpool lane and act very smug with our children and our contemporaries. We are in the "in" crowd even if no one else knows or cares! Actually we are beyond the "in" crowd: We now have two hybrids.

For the record, I've still kept my dream car. My 1995 Jaguar XJS is my fantasy blue convertible, and I will never sell it. I learned that lesson the hard way when I sold my 1965 blue convertible Mustang in order to buy a station wagon to chauffeur my kids around in. My grandkids, still comparatively innocent of environmental concerns, love my Jag almost as much as I do. We always keep the top down so that whenever the weather is good, which is most days in California, we can sneak off and go "cruising with Granny."

On my radio show recently, I was able to do an interview with Honda featuring their FCX Clarity Hydrogen Vehicle. It was an amazing trip into the future with a car that has *zero* emissions. Now there is a new dream car in my future.

Unlike their parents, none of our children have bought hybrids yet. I think they are waiting for us to move up on the FCX waiting list. Then they plan to inherit our out-dated hybrids, especially the one with a carpool lane sticker that is no longer available.

Isn't it grand to have accidentally ecologically correct parents?

Chapter Four

Couples

It is so wonderful to finally team up with someone who will stand by you through all of life's trials and tribulations, but the reality is that you would never have had any of those particular trials and tribulations had you never met that one special person. Marriage may thrive on commitment, but like insanity, it can also lead to being committed.

My favorite annoying new couples' trend is the promise ring, which is great for those wishy-washy duos who really don't know if they're right for each other or if they want to make that final commitment, and the plague of all mothers who live to plan big weddings.

In my opinion, the hardest part of becoming a couple after you take marriage vows is that it can drastically change a relationship. You start out falling in love and going to bed with your best friend, who is also your one and only lover. Then you wake up one morning to find out that you're sleeping next to your nearest relative. And he snores!

> **Men who have a pierced ear are better prepared for marriage: they've experienced pain and bought jewelry.**
>
> —*Rita Rudner*

Top Ten
Couples' Whines

#1 Money
#2 Jobs
#3 Each Other – Stage One
#4 Each Other – Stage Two
#5 In-laws
#6 Sharing Chores
#7 Entertaining
#8 Lack of Romance
#9 Closet Space
#10 Pillows

Before marriage, a man declares that he would lay down his life
to serve you; after marriage, he won't even lay down
his newspaper to talk to you.

—*Helen Rowland*

1
Money

> **Matrimony is a process by which
> a grocer acquires an account the florist once had.**
>
> —*Francis Rodman*

Whine A: I need more! What did you do with it?

Why: Lack of money is one of those universal whines that couples young and old alike can share. There never seems to be enough money for all the little things required to feather the proverbial nest or to keep any healthy couple well-fed and entertained. This has been a problem ever since couples began cohabitating, and it can be especially frustrating for the increasing number of families who bring in two incomes and still don't have enough money.

Whine B: We can't afford it.

Cure: The only way to deal with this situation is to do the **"cut up the credit cards"** cure. This can be a very brutal method to manage your money. The cash-only policy is an effective way to control spending that is too simple and clear to argue against: When you run out of cash, then you stop spending. Obviously, this is not a popular cure for the "instant gratification generation." In fact, cutting up cards can be downright hazardous to both your health and your marriage if both of you don't agree to do it at the same time for the same reasons. Just ask any divorce lawyer.

2
Jobs

> **Many marriages are simply working partnerships between businessmen and housekeepers.**
>
> *—Mignon McLaughlin*

Whine A: I hate my job.

Why: It is nothing short of a miracle when a person is able to find the perfect job for the perfect amount of compensation; and the rest of us are left to whine about our less ideal positions. Jobs are an even bigger issue now that most couples are two-income entities. Everybody's main complaint, of course, is that they don't get paid enough for what they do. With partners in a relationship both working, it just doubles the trouble. It is a difficult task to go to work at a job that you hate. Sadly, discontent in the workplace has become a way of life for many.

Whine B: Why do I have to work so hard?

Cure: The **"be your own boss"** cure is the ideal answer, but it is easier said than done. If you can't start your own business, try to do something part-time that you love doing. Try to find your passion, no matter what it may be. I do not mean sex, drugs or rock 'n' roll. Those are merely escapes, while what I'm suggesting is a real, soul-fulfilling cure. Once you are doing what you love, or even if you're doing something on your own steam that is not what you love but nonetheless much less loathsome than working meaninglessly for someone else ever was—and even if it doesn't make you rich—it will make you happy despite yourself.

3
Each Other – Stage One

Marriage is an alliance entered into by a man who can't sleep with the window shut and a woman who can't sleep with the window open.

—*George Bernard Shaw*

Whine A: She/he drives me crazy.

Why: Whining about each other is an age-old ritual that is common to most marriages. It is an unavoidable part of most partnerships, and many would even consider it a healthy part. It's also very easy to whine about your spouse to your friends because most people have the same problems with their spouses that you do. Whining goes with any couples' territory, as spouses tend to develop ingenious ways of irritating each other on a daily basis.

Whine B: He doesn't help at home.

Cure: The **"go to a couples shrink"** cure is the most effective way to deal with spousal whining. I know most couples will respond by saying they can't afford to go for counseling. Well, I'm here to tell you that you can't afford not to go. Better to give your hard-earned money to a counselor of your choice than the divorce lawyer your spouse chooses to take you to the cleaners.

4
Each Other – Stage Two

> I love being married.
> It's so great to find that one special person
> you want to annoy for the rest of your life.
>
> —*Rita Rudner*

Whine A: He's a jerk. She's an idiot.

Why: I guess when couples reach whining of grandiose proportions, it can only be chalked up to the differences between the male and female of the species. Both men and women have their own instinctual approaches to life that are usually in exact opposition to the others'. Also, you must factor in the reality that some people are not happy unless they are unhappy. They basically adore disagreeing. Generally, this type of person is attracted to someone who is on the same page; it is their reason for living.

Whine B: I can't talk sense to you.

Cure: The **"let's agree to disagree"** cure is the only one that works with some couples who simply can't seem to stop bickering about even the smallest of differences in perception. If you can't agree to disagree, then you will spend the rest of your life arguing with each other. As mentioned above, there are those masochists among us who enjoy such contention in a relationship; but if you find yourself in this type of relationship and don't necessarily relish waging war about every little thing at any given moment, you'd better learn to be very quiet, or very quietly get out of town.

5
In-Laws

Whine A: I can't stand her/his mother.

Why: The in-law whine, like most family complaints, probably began with the first marriages in the Garden of Eden; however, the logistics of this has always been problematic for me since Adam and Eve only had two sons and no daughters. In any case, in-law complaints are not only for mother-in-laws since they can be aimed at father-in-laws, siblings, grandparents, aunts, uncles, and all the rest with equal severity. It is very hard to do damage control in sticky situations between parents-in-law and their children-in-law—especially if you are one of those rare mothers-in-law with only the best of intentions, like me.

Whine B: Can't they mind their own business?

Cure: The **"mind your own business"** cure is indeed the only one that works. It can be brutal sometimes, but necessary. Do ask yourself before using it if you are willing to sacrifice gratis babysitting to make a point. This cure could burn some bridges that you might need to cross again in the future, so be careful: Your Saturday Night Live could become your Saturday Night Dead without a free and usually available babysitter.

6
Sharing Chores

I've been married to one Marxist and one Fascist, and
neither one would take the garbage out.

—*Lee Grant*

Whine A: You don't do your share.

Why: The division of labor in two-income homes is one of the most
challenging aspects of modern day marriage or cohabitation. There
never is enough time to get all the chores done around the house
with two worker bees busy in the hive all day. This is an especially
aggravating whine for stay-at-home mothers, who are often treated like
hourly-wage housekeepers rather than full-share, working partners.
Whining about their apparent lack of input can make them feel that
their efforts are not appreciated or even noticed, leading to resentment
and, eventually, even further whining.

Whine B: Why do I have to do everything?

Cure: The **"nobody plays or rests"** cure until everybody plays
or rests can work well. It is commonly known as job sharing. Quite
simply, it means you do your share of the chores or else both of you
will be miserable for a very, long time. In marriage years, this could be
longer than an eternity.

7
Entertaining

> **Like good wine, marriage gets better with age,**
> **once you learn to keep a cork in it.**
>
> —*Gene Perret*

Whine A: I hate having your family over.

Why: Entertaining as a couple can be a delight or a disaster. It all depends on the couple's state of mind and willingness to make it work. Unless you are a Martha Stewart clone, it is hard to entertain without some sort of help. Sometimes entertaining can be mandatory and that makes it a really unpleasant experience. The command performance drills that families go through are brutal. Just ask my kids.

Whine B: Why do I have to do all the work?

Cure: The **"let's have some fun or not do it at all"** cure is my personal favorite for this situation. This works when all parties involved in hosting an event have the same agenda; and what agenda should any entertainer or group of entertainers ever have but to have fun and to make sure their guests are doing the same? If you can't have fun doing this as a couple, than put a time-out on trying to host or impress anyone, especially your in-laws. But be judicious and realistic: I know of some time-outs that have lasted longer than the marriages that prompted them in the first place!

8

Lack of Romance

Whine A: I'm too tired.

Why: The lack of romance in most relationships is due to a lack of time, energy and/or incentive. There's never enough time for anything, let alone intimacy; energy is a problem because usually one or both of you are exhausted; and lack of incentive can easily come about when the same old routine of romance becomes an unromantic chore. Couples can get very complacent about romance and sex, letting them fall by the wayside like unpicked blossoms; or they can mix the two up until no one knows what to do, and cares even less whether they do it or not..

Whine B: I have a headache.

Cure: The **"let's get crazy"** cure will definitely improve both your romantic and your sexual relationship. Try to do something neither of you have ever done before. It can be anything, from innocent details like a change in time or location to more intimate arrangements like the addition of toys or other romantic innovations. Anything goes as long as it's not a different partner altogether, which can be very exciting, but very expensive—especially after your divorce takes place.

9
Closet Space

Whine A: Your stuff's on my side.

Why: When a couple shares anything, it can be tricky. This is especially true of closet space. Sadly, there is no closet on earth that can blissfully accommodate both a woman and a man. This is one of the laws of nature of which most people, especially newlyweds, are not aware. This law came into effect when the world was created—no, actually, it could have happened only when Eve arrived: She told Adam to clear his fig leaves out of their tree-house closet because she needed more space, and she needed it right away. And why did she need this extra space despite her equally unimpressive wardrobe? Because she was a woman, of course!

Whine B: How many shoes do you need?

Cure: The **"separate closet"** cure is the one and only one that works for most couples. It insures that neither partner has any idea of what goes on in, or into, the other's side of the wardrobe world. Some things are not ever meant to be shared, and closet space, in my opinion, is certainly one of these. If you have no space or amenities for separate closets, at least you can attempt to use your joint closet at separate times, thereby circumventing the urge to whine while your spouse is busy getting ready for work or some other time-sensitive commitment.

10
Pillows

Whine A: *My wife won't let me touch them.*

Why: Pillows are a battleground in most marriages and some relationships. The reason for this is that most women love to put them on their beds—lots of them—while most men love to throw them on the floor. God forbid that any man should try to put them back on the bed in the morning. This is absolutely not allowed since there is no way on earth they could do it correctly. No matter how hard they try, the placement will not be acceptable to their respective wives. It will have to be done over by her the minute she sees them on the bed, and that's just a fact of life.

Whine B: *Why do we have so many?*

Cure: The **"eight pillow"** cure is one that my husband developed over the years. It came about after he asked all the men he knew how many pillows were on their beds, and whether they were ever allowed to touch them. Most had to ask their wives how many they actually had, but they all knew without asking that they were not to ever touch them. After his survey, we both decided that eight pillows was not so many as to make a man crazy, and not so few as to make a woman feel like her bed is unfinished, uncomfortable and unattractive.

Best Overall Cure
for Whining Couples

The Echo Effect or
Return to Sender Cure

This is an interesting cure that may not be effective with some couples since it could possibly be grounds for divorce or murder. It probably would be best used with children or people who are much smaller than you. The Echo Effect, also known as the Return to Sender Cure, is a simple process of repeating everything the whiner says to you. You must use the same words, the same cadence and the same tone. The results will amaze you. By verbally returning the whine to the sender, you will gradually disarm the whiner.

This repetition will annoy the whiner, but it may also open them to the silliness of the situation, leading to a non-stop, ever-escalating volley of quick-served whines. If this procedure is humorously done, it can result in laughter producing a real bonding experience. Recently on my radio show, I interviewed some experts on laughing. You can go to my archive at www.januaryjones.com and learn all about The World Laughter Tour and Laughing Yoga.

Just a quick warning—the "return to sender" cure, unless employed with all due care, can backfire, creating two whiners instead of one. Not good!

Chapter Five

Singles

You can't really appreciate how wonderful it is to be a single entity until you are stuck in traffic with a car full of whining kids or caught having dinner at Chuck E. Cheese—for the third time in the same week. The reality is that singles often think they have something to whine about when their complaints couldn't possibly hold a candle to those of their married counterparts.

When singles whine about growing old and being alone, for instance, I usually suggest that they get a pet, or better yet, several of them. There are so many smart people who are settling on pets these days instead of human life partners. Pets are always glad to see you, they never talk back and they are always there when you need them as long as you feed them regularly.

The un-coupling of our most advanced societies is a phenomenon that is escalating as more and more young people discover that they'd rather keep the joys and freedoms of the single life than tie themselves down. If you are a part of this evolutionary movement, you'd better be prepared to deal with disapproval—the kind that will come from all of your family and friends who can't figure out how you became so much smarter than them.

> **There are easier things in life than finding a good man.
> Nailing Jell-O to a tree, for instance.**
>
> —*Single Women Everywhere*

Top Ten
Singles' Whines

#1   Money

#2   Love Life

#3   Jobs

#4   Bills

#5   Cost of Living

#6   Weight

#7   Bad Hair Days

#8   Blind Dates

#9   Lack of Sleep

#10 Boredom

By all means use some time to be alone.

—*George Herbert*

1
Money

> **I am opposed to millionaires,
> but it would be dangerous to offer me the position.**
>
> —*Mark Twain*

Whine A: I need more.

Why: Most singles are desperately in need of more money to support their lifestyles. It seems impossible for a single person, with no one to share the burden, to keep up with the cost of living anymore, what with rent, car payments, utilities, clothes, food, entertainment, dating expenses and the cruel interest charged for using all those convenient credit cards to live beyond one's means. Everyone needs money for the necessities of life, but for some reason the single set is more distressed about it. They certainly haven't bought into the myth that two can live as cheaply as one.

Whine B: I'm broke again! Where does it go?

Cure: The **"get a second job"** cure has worked well for many people. This is harder for singles to attempt since they have time constraints due to dating. This cure actually works better when you are in a relationship and the other person gets the second job. If that's not possible, then you have to suck it up by spending less or working more. No one said it was going to be easy, and it isn't.

2
Love Life

You have to walk carefully in the beginning of love; the running across fields into your lover's arms can only come later when you're sure they won't laugh if you trip.

—*Jonathan Carroll*

Whine A: I don't have one.

Why: The supposedly bountiful love life of singles is a wondrous mystery to most people, including the singles themselves. Finding the right person and trying to maintain a relationship can be frustrating, depressing, downright discouraging; and playing the field can be especially perilous in today's world of sexual promiscuity. It's not easy no matter what age or gender you might be, and it never has been, but nowadays it sure does seem a bit harder to find that special someone, despite the supposed ease of Internet compatibility services and the like.

Whine B: Why don't I have one?

Cure: The **"jump right in and get your feet wet"** cure works wonders for those who are willing to give it a try. Remember that you have nothing to lose except your pride, and that you have a lot to gain if you can actually find someone with whom you share a natural—and exciting—connection. If true love isn't just waiting around for you somewhere obvious, you might as well have some fun looking for it in all the wrong places. It is the ultimate hide-and-seek game for all ages.

3
Jobs

> **Accomplishing the impossible means only that the boss will add it to your regular duties.**
>
> —*Doug Larson*

Whine A: I hate my job.

Why: Today's workplace is treacherous terrain to travel. The competition is fierce, and it really is a dog-eat-dog dilemma on a daily basis. Finding a job that pays well and offers appropriate benefits is essential to your survival—and it's not easy or even enjoyable to find your passion or purpose in life when you have to worry all the time about your basic survival.

Whine B: I hate my boss.

Cure: The **"find your passion"** cure is one of the most effective and most difficult to administer. Doing something you love is crucial when thinking in terms of a lifetime occupation. If you can't find the right job, hang in there, because not to do so would mean you were out of the game. You need to keep on playing in order to eventually win. No one sitting on the bench has ever been the hero who hit the homerun that won the game.

4
Bills

> **If you think nobody cares if you are alive,
> try missing a couple of car payments.**
>
> —*Earl Wilson*

Whine A: I'll never get out of debt.

Why: Being in debt is a fact of life and a way of life for many people, no matter who they are or what their circumstances. Unfortunately, the "buy now, pay later" mentality is in overdrive even though it seems to have run its viable course. It all seems so simple at first. Then the reality of high interest payments takes over and you are screwed. For many singles it starts right on our college campuses, where credit card companies are passing cards out like candy to all the cash-poor, unsuspecting co-eds.

Whine B: I owe everybody.

Cure: The **"make a budget and live by it"** cure is one way to rope in your own runaway debt. Another more drastic measure is my favorite old money-oriented stand-by, the "cut up the credit cards" cure. This is certainly an avenue to consider traveling when you are in debt over your head, and while I have never been able to do it myself, I am told it is very effective.

5
Cost of Living

> Inflation hasn't ruined everything.
> A dime can still be used as a screwdriver.
>
> —H. Jackson Browne, Jr.

Whine A: Everything's so expensive.

Why: It is just a fact that the cost of living has been going up steadily throughout time, and there's no abatement of this trend in sight. Everyone is in the same boat, but it seems that few singles are able to stay ahead or even keep up with the rat race due to lack of support in other areas of their lives. This is especially perilous for seniors who live on a fixed income. Many have had their pensions cut back by large companies circumventing bankruptcies and puffing up wimpy bottom lines with other people's money. Now that's something to *really* whine about.

Whine B: I can't keep up. It's insane.

Cure: Sadly, the **"spend less"** cure is the only one that will work for this whine. It is a brutal one since most people are already simply trying to make it one day at a time. Now is the time to think of the things in your life that are your real wealth—those things that no amount of money could ever buy. Of course, it also helps to cultivate and wisely distribute both self-control and will power when attempting this most complicated and uncomfortable of cures.

6
Weight

> **A diet is the penalty we pay
> for exceeding the feed limit.**
>
> —*January Jones*

Whine A: *I'm so fat.*

Why: This is a whine shared by all sorts of singles of all ages and all backgrounds. It is fueled by our material, vain culture, which values slimness above health or self-esteem. Designers and advertisers use stick-thin models to sell their clothes, making anyone else who attempts to wear them feel like a fat slob. Historically, it has been women who whine most about their weight, but men are increasingly joining the choir of voices who constantly sing a song of unattainable sveltitude. In this world so bent on physical perfection at all cost, mirrors can be anyone's enemy.

Whine B: *I can't lose weight. How did you do it?*

Cure: The **"find the right diet for you"** cure is the path to follow when trying to lose weight. This is a quest that may take a lifetime. An even better cure is to live a healthy, sensible life nourished by a sustainable diet that suits your body type. This is sage advice I am still only attempting to follow after more years than I want to admit. Like many of the most basic and logical things in life, it is also one of those tasks that is far easier said than done.

7
Bad Hair Days

Whine A: My hair's a mess.

Why: This is mostly a women's issue, but it's a big one with many facets. A bad hair day can be caused by a multitude of mishaps: It could be due to a bad cut or bad color or bad shampoo. Bad hair can mean bad frizz, bad straight, bad curly, bad thin, bad thick, bad weather or bad whatever. For men a bad hair day is usually connected to a rough night in the sack. Men tend to wake up with some of the most ridiculous hairdos imaginable. It is called "bed head," and they seem to thoroughly enjoy it, even going so far as to use hair products to simulate the look when it's not happening in a natural way.

Whine B: I need a good haircut.

Cure: The **"find a good hairdresser"** cure will take care of this whine. It is never easy to find your own special hairdresser, but it is the only solution. Be prepared for many disappointments along the way, and remember that you should never give up on this quest. As for men who experience bad hair days, try the **"shave your head"** cure—it's so "in." If you are already bald, the good news is that bald is the new hot.

8
Blind Dates

| 1 | 1 | 1 | 1 | 1 | 1 | 1 |

> **The hunger for love is much more difficult
> to remove than the hunger for bread.**
>
> —*Mother Teresa*

Whine A: What's he/she like?

Why: Welcome to the wonderful world of blind dating—so called because this sector of the mating game always seems like it's full of the blind leading the blind. Most people who are single are bombarded by their married friends with fix-up prospects. This is because they can't stand seeing anyone who is unattached living such a happy, carefree life. The "misery loves company" cliché is an accurate description of the blind dating scene, and of those who set up such doomed-to-fail events for their undeserving friends.

Whine B: They never work out. Why bother?

Cure: The **"meet for coffee"** cure is one method that I wholeheartedly endorse. This way you can both look each other over without a lot of expense or emotional trauma. It is best to only subject yourself to blind dates with people who are highly recommended by friends you trust, though you must always keep in mind that all blind dates can be perilous no matter how pure the source. They can be especially dangerous if the date is someone from your best friend's family. You know—the one with that *great* personality everybody's always talking so much about...

9
Lack of Sleep & Exhaustion

1	1	1	1	1	1	1

> Laughter and tears are both responses
> to frustration and exhaustion.
> I myself prefer to laugh, since there
> is less cleaning up to do afterward.
>
> —*Kurt Vonnegut*

Whine A: I'm exhausted.

Why: Most singles are exhausted because they lead lives that most of us can only dream about. They are the ones out there on the front lines who are partying, playing and putting out. They are the chosen ones for their generation to carry the torch of youth into middle age and beyond. Nobody said it would be easy, but someone has got to do it; and frankly, as glamorous as it sounds from afar, I'm glad it's them and not me.

Whine B: I can't sleep.

Cure: The **"party on"** cure for whining about exhaustion is universally accepted as the only one for singles, at least those singles who are young enough at heart—and body, for that matter—to stand it. No matter what their age or physical shape, however, singles generally rule supreme when it comes to the social scene. Lack of sleep is the price they must pay for their playtime. No one feels sorry for them; everyone's actually just envious, an emotion that even plenty of rest can't quench.

10
Boredom

1 1 1 1 1 1 1

> **Grasp your opportunities
> no matter how poor your health;
> nothing is worse for your health than boredom.**
>
> —*Mignon McLaughlin*

Whine A: I'm so bored.

Why: Singles whine about boredom because they can. When you have only yourself to think about, it is easy to be bored with life. You do not have to consider other people or their problems as you explore life's mysteries. It is the one station of life in which you have only one concern: you. There are no worries about spouses, kids, in-laws or the rest of those issues that so bedevil couples. Being bored is a sign that you are on the right track to a stress-free single life.

Whine B: There's nothing to do.

Cure: The best treatment for the boredom whine is the **"don't change a thing"** cure. Why ruin a good thing? Just keep on thinking about yourself, and then when something or someone intriguing comes along, you will be ready. When you are single, it is okay to be bored, especially if you are alone. Also, it is very important to always remember that it is all right to be bored as long as you are never boring.

Best Overall Cure
for Whining Singles

The One Second,
One Word Quick Cure

This cure is one that can help anyone who is stuck on himself or herself, single or not, to start thinking about others, or at least to pretend that they are interested in someone other than themselves. It's also a good way to meet someone you might enjoy getting to know, which can never be a bad thing when you're single.

To stop self-centered whining before it starts, all you need to do is to eliminate one word from your vocabulary: **I**! It will only take one second to get rid of one word for a quick cure.

When you think about it, every conversation that ends up a whine usually starts with the word **I**. For example: "I don't want to...", "I don't like it," or "I want it my way." If you can stop saying **I**, it will stop you from whining. Without **I** in the wh "I"ne , most complaining is irrelevant.

What would I suggest doing instead of whining about your own unworthy obsessions? How about starting every sentence with a question addressed to the other person. Try asking them about the who, what, where, when or why in their lives. Their answers will be more interesting than you can imagine. New knowledge gained this way stimulates the brain waves and makes for a more fulfilling and healthful life, or so **"I"** am told.

Chapter Six

Baby Boomers

①⑨④⑥—①⑨⑥④

Baby Boomers were born to whine. They are to whining what computers are to crashing. They couldn't exist with out it. All Boomers want to be winners but usually they end up whiners.

My Baby Boomer friends, myself included, are the instant gratification generation. If we see it, we've got to have it. Even if we don't know what it is, what it will do or how it will do it, we still have to have it. A classic example is my iPhone. It is an instant way to get attention and impress whomever I need to impress.

The most impressive thing to me about my phone is when I'm actually am able to work it. The best advice I can give to all Baby Boomers is to find a new friend who is the geekiest, savviest techie person in your world. Your new best friend will probably be a teenager, so be prepared to spend a lot of time and money at the Apple Store or playing Wii with them.

Once you become an Apple Addict and buy your iPhone, it is like joining a secret cult. All iPhoners want to do is talk to other iPhoners because they speak the same language. There's not much to whine about here except for the outrageous amount of attitude you will have to keep up as part of the Appleholic crowd.

> **I personally believe we have developed language because of our deep inner need to complain.**
>
> *—Jane Wagner*

Top Ten
Baby Boomers' Whines
❶❾❹❻—❶❾❻❹

#1	Money
#2	Jobs
#3	Love Life
#4	Computers & Cell Phones
#5	Fitness
#6	Taxes
#7	Aging
#8	Weight
#9	Kids
#10	Slow Old(er) Drivers

Age is an issue of mind over matter.
If you don't mind, it doesn't matter.

—*Mark Twain*

1
Money

①⑨④⑥—①⑨⑥④

> When I was young I thought that money
> was the most important thing in life;
> now that I am old I *know* that it is.
>
> —*Oscar Wilde*

Whine A: Where did it all go?

Why: Baby boomers whine about money just like everyone else, only more so. It's difficult to make ends meet day to day. Then before you know it, you are getting ready to think about retirement, suddenly realizing it's closer than you think. Just when you have finished educating your kids, it is time to review your ever-dwindling finances once again. Time flies when you're having fun. Unfortunately, so does your money.

Whine B: I can't make ends meet.

Cure: The **"start planning your retirement right now...no, I mean *right* now"** cure is the most expedient for baby boomers who whine about money. You need to have your finances in order because time is running out. You need an exit plan that will take you up to your final departure, and I don't mean on a plane or train. Life is terminal, and not having enough funds for the grand finale is neither fun nor funny. And if you simply can't get serious about saving for your twilight years, you can always follow my lead and plan on winning the lottery.

2
Jobs

①⑨④⑥—①⑨⑥④

> **It is better to have a permanent income than to be fascinating.**
>
> —*Oscar Wilde*

Whine A: I hate my job.

Why: Many baby boomers get stuck in jobs that they hate. It starts out with a temporary position that somehow becomes a lifetime career. You may think you'll eventually find your dream job, but life somehow seems to keep getting in the way of every little opportunity. For baby boomers still raising families, it's extremely difficult and risky to make career changes unless absolutely necessary, as in the case of downsizing or dismissal. When there's no choice, you have to make a change, and hopefully it will be for the better. Until then, if you're a good, pragmatic, security-loving baby boomer, you'll just have to keep on whining about that job you hate.

Whine B: My boss is a jerk.

Cure: The **"find your passion and do it as soon as humanly possible"** cure would be my best advice to work-weary baby boomers. As it is for anyone else, though, this is easier said than done. I never found mine until I was in my fifties. I became a writer with her first book on the front of *The National Enquirer*. Talk about scary. Some boomers find their passion on golf courses or in senior's softball leagues. That's certainly fine, as long as you have already saved enough for retirement to play away the rest of your days—just in case you don't get called up to the Majors.

3
Love Life

①⑨④⑥—①⑨⑥④

Money and women!
They're two of the strongest things in the world. The things you
do for a woman you wouldn't do for anything else.
Same with money.

—Satchel Paige

Whine A: I'm too tired.

Why: Most baby boomers can probably admit that they are beginning to experience a deceleration of their sex drives. Sometimes, it is because they are just too tired or not in the mood, but they may also simply have never found the right partner. And even if you have found the one for you, it is hard to keep the passion burning with its initial fury, especially when you have been together forever and a trillion days.

Whine B: I have a headache.

Cure: The **"Viagra"** cure can guarantee a romantic evening. This is one of the most widely used drugs in existence today, yet there are not many men who will admit they need it or use it, except for my husband. Actually, we both have tried it. Whether you need it or not, we both highly recommend it, especially if you want a prolonged evening of enjoyment with a happy ending. If that doesn't work for you then you both can just OD on chocolate together.

4

Computers and Cell Phones

❶❾❹❻—❶❾❻❹

> **Never let a computer know you're in a rush.**
>
> —*John Gabbey, III*

Whine A: My reception is terrible.

Why: Computers and cell phones are with us to stay, but that doesn't mean that they won't succeed in driving a very large number of us crazy in the meantime. From cell phones with bad reception to computers that are always crashing, technology takes it toll on baby boomers, who mostly came to these technologies later in their lives, thus making it more difficult for them to easily adapt. For me, it has now become impossible to keep up with all the new gadgets that come out since they seem to change almost daily in order to keep up with the planned obsolescence factor. You know, the one that greedy corporations have devised in order to keep us buying new cell phones, for instance, before we can even figure out how to use our old ones.

Whine B: It's so annoying.

Cure: The **"smash or unplug it"** cure is the one most baby boomers secretly wish they could do without losing their jobs or their lives. Buckeye Leif's phone has become a permanent appendage that incessantly plays the Ohio State fight song. I, for one, wish we could go back to the carefree days when we only answered the phone if it rang when we were home, and only experts and programmers were allowed to touch anything computerized.

5
Fitness

①⑨④⑥—①⑨⑥④

Those who think they have not time for
bodily exercise will sooner or later
have to find time for illness.

—*Edward Stanley*

Whine A: I'm so out of shape.

Why: Staying fit is nearly impossible for most baby boomers simply because there isn't enough time in the day. Between working and raising a family, there's no time or motivation to follow a fitness regime as well. Besides, most of us hate working out more than we will ever admit. The fitness craze is better suited to younger people who are single or on the prowl. For them, the gym has replaced going to church; for baby boomers, it can be more like purgatory.

Whine B: I joined a gym but never go.

Cure: The **"find a workout buddy"** cure is the only pleasant way I have found to commit to a regular fitness program. The ideal buddy would be your spouse, life partner or current flame, but in a pinch, a best friend can get you off your butt and working out again, too. Basically, you should look for anyone who can make you feel guilty about your growing gut or sagging butt; however, under no circumstances should this be your mother or your father.

6

Taxes

①⑨④⑥—①⑨⑥④

> **Inflation is taxation without representation.**
>
> —*Milton Friedman*

Whine A: The rich get richer.

Why: Nobody enjoys paying taxes, and most people resent the amount they must pay. On top of that, boomers generally seem to feel that the government is not run as well as it could be. They resent their tax dollars flowing uselessly into ineffective programs. Lately, paying for an unpopular war really has been upsetting most taxpayers, but this especially goads boomers because their younger, more pliable minds were first formed in a time when many people were pushing the abolishment of war forever as more than an ideal. Taxes are just barely tolerable when they are used for development instead of destruction, so who's to stop boomers if they want to whine about footing the bill for an endless and indecisive armed conflict?

Whine B: Why can't I write this off?

Cure: The **"get an honest accountant"** cure is my preferred method of dealing with taxation. So far, our accountant has been a big help with our taxes; at least he has kept us all out of jail. Tax time can be stressful unless you know that extensions are not just telephone outlets, and this, among others, are the sorts of informative tidbits you will learn from an honest-to-goodness, hard-working, numbers-crunching, assets-claiming, no-nonsense tax accountant.

7
Aging

①⑨④⑥—①⑨⑥④

> Growing old is mandatory;
> growing up is optional.
>
> —*Chili Davis*

Whine A: I look like a prune.

Why: Simply put, no matter how old you are or how old you feel, aging is not fun for anyone. It's not for sissies or for most baby boomers. People tend to remember their years of youth as their glory days, the best days of their lives. This creates a pervasive sadness in an aging population with such an overwhelming nostalgia for the way things were, as the boomers have shown us in their literature and cinema. Aging can't be changed or avoided, so it's a total frustration. Baby boomers are America's next senior citizens. This cruel reality is not a pleasant one to even ponder for anybody who still has some spark left in them.

Whine B: Botox costs too much.

Cure: The **"get over it and get a life"** cure is suggested for baby boomers who whine about aging. Everyone agrees aging's a pain in the butt, but considering the alternatives, it's best to suck it up and keep on keepin' on. Our desired goal is to attempt to age without becoming a total bitch of an old lady or pain-in-the-ass geezer. Baby boomers who can stop whining long enough to smell the roses should think about planting a few wild seeds instead of just rotating the crops. Going over the same territory again and again can etch unflattering wrinkles into your face and make you look old!

8
Weight

❶❾❹❻—❶❾❻❹

> **Never eat more than you can lift.**
>
> —*Miss Piggy*

Whine A: I can't lose weight.

Why: Unfortunately for most of us, society values thinness and not fleshiness. Thin is in! (Was it ever out?) We see its avatars every day, slim and serene and powerful in our movies and magazines. This is not just a problem for baby boomers, but for our entire population. Being overweight carries with it many health dangers, and the less you weigh the longer your life expectancy, or so they say; but our current labeling of any but those who border on emaciated as "too big" has certainly taken this issue way too far.

Whine B: I can't stay on this diet.

Cure: The **"get lipo"** cure is one of my favorites, but it is a costly solution not available to everyone. Unless you can afford to get your fat sucked out of you by a trained professional, the only real solution to your flab problem is to eat less and exercise more. Personally I advocate the **"Curves"** cure for a fun work out. for women. Where else can you have your own computerized, totally discreet personal trainer who can't yell at you? Whatever you do, the point is to have fun doing it. My husband and I once did the Martinis and Whipped Cream Diet, and we loved it. Once we had a couple of martinis, we'd forget all about eating. As for the whipped cream, you can either eat it straight from a spoon or enjoy it in bed before you both pass out.

9
Kids

①⑨④⑥—①⑨⑥④

> **Cleaning your house while your kids
> are still growing up is like
> shoveling the walk before it stops snowing.**
>
> —*Phyllis Diller*

Whine A: What were we thinking?

Why: Why do baby boomers whine about their children? Well let me tell you, most kids are the result of the opportunity to have sex. After the sex is over, the real fun starts. People think that their kids will provide them with companionship in their old age, which rarely happens unless they are very wealthy. I've been told that some kids actually like their parents, and that a select few will even admit to loving them. Don't get too excited, though—they would still rather be with their friends or foes than with their folks.

Whine B: I'm too young to be a grandparent.

Cure: The **"glad I got it over with early, at least"** cure is the only sure way to stop whining about your kids and their kids and all the mistakes you've all made. If you started a family recklessly early like many baby boomers, you can now safely laugh at the Gen-X fools who are having carefully planned babies at the age of 40 or more. While they're still paying for their kids' educations, you'll already be watching your children struggle to pay your grandchildren's exorbitant college fees—while you golf with your business partners or relax on some faraway beach.

10
Slow, Old(er) Drivers
①⑨④⑥—①⑨⑥④

> Patience is something you admire in the driver behind you and scorn in the one ahead.
>
> —Mac McCleary

Whine A: Why can't the old farts merge?

Why: It is important to remember that slow drivers can come in all ages, all sexes and all sizes, and they can be irritating, dangerous and frustrating all at once. Who hasn't wanted to ram a brake-riding slowpoke in the rear end out of sheer impatience, especially when already running late? This is a favorite whine of baby boomers due to the fact that most of them are always in a hurry, and often forget that they will be old themselves before they know it.

Whine B: They shouldn't have a license.

Cure: The **"beep your horn, that's what it's for"** cure works well sometimes, or it can backfire, making the slow driver even slower. This is a tough call to make if you don't want to cause an accident or commit murder. If they are older drivers, they possibly won't even hear your horn. When you are behind a snail-slow driver, whatever you do, don't resort to verbal abuse or run them off the road. This is important especially if they are bigger than you.

Best Overall Cure
for Whining Baby Boomers

The High School
Reunion Cure

Baby Boomers can get so caught up in the here and now that they can easily lose track of old friends, especially when they move away from their hometowns. The Time Machine factor takes over and you are thrust into the future with no looking back.

Then, before you know it, you are invited back for your 10th high school reunion. This one is the easiest to skip. "You've got to be kidding me," you might hear yourself say, "ten years already? It's not possible. It seems like we just graduated. I'll go to the next one when I've made my millions and lost twenty pounds. Maybe I'll even be married with kids by then."

Then, before you know it *again*, your 20th reunion has arrived. All the baby boomers who are on track go to this one. It's fun to see everyone again and compare notes, share baby pictures and tell tall tales about your life so far. You think it's amazing because everyone still looks pretty good for their age, especially you.

And then, suddenly and unbelievably, it's time for your 25th reunion. This is the big one. You even start dieting and working out for this one six months in advance. This is a not-to-be-missed opportunity for any boomers who are divorced to reconnect with their high school sweethearts, particularly if the old flame turns out to be divorced too.

By the time you get to your 30th and 40th reunion, none of your old friends will show up. Instead, all of their parents will be there. You will meet a lot of really old people who vaguely remind you of people you used to know a long time ago. How can this be? You're still the same. What happened to all of them?

If you are a Baby Boomer or a Sexy Senior and lucky enough to have a class reunion, don't hesitate to go. It will be one of the most amazing things you will ever do. You will step back into the time machine to relive things that you had completely forgotten.

The best part is the unconditional love that you will feel. No one judges anymore because we are all too old for such silly things. If only those young girls back then could have been then like the women they are now. If only they could have known the things they know now.

We all know it doesn't work that way. Nobody gets the perfect life, even the ones you thought would do so. All of us have had our share of tears and pain. No need to look back. That's why the windshield of a car is so big and the rearview mirrors are so small. And that's why, after a few glasses of wine, I promised I'd mention all my former classmates in my next book. Unfortunately, I can't remember any of their names!

Immaculata Class of 1961
45th Reunion Attendees:
You know who you are!

Chapter Seven

Seniors

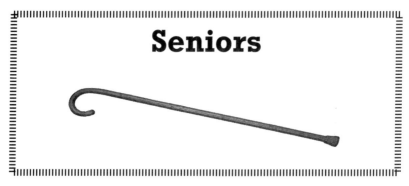

Seniors and whining go together like prunes and constipation. It is so challenging for some seniors to keep up with the ever-accelerating changes in the world these days that some of them never find time to do anything but whine, especially about things that were better the way they were before than they are now.

One of these is usually their income, which has often gone way down from what they were used to. People spend their entire lives waiting for the day they will have money to burn, and it never arrives because they have either run out or burned out too soon. When they grow old and attempt to live on the dreaded "fixed income" they find out quickly that it's awfully nice to get out of the rat race but damned hard to get along with less cheese.

Seniors also adore whining about their health but can't seem to get around to doing anything to get better. The fact is that they will do anything to improve except to give up the problem. Besides, it's fun to whine with other seniors. By this time of their lives, they have made an art of it, and it's certainly one that thrives on being explored and shared with other seniors who have just as much to whine about, and just about as much energy to do it.

> **A man is as old as he's feeling.**
> **A woman is as old as she looks.**
>
> —*Mortimer Collins*

Top Ten
Seniors' Whines

#1 Money

#2 Aging

#3 Loneliness

#4 Losing things

#5 Forgetting things

#6 Health

#7 Boredom

#8 Retirement

#9 Dying

#10 Insomnia

People who don't cherish their elderly have forgotten
whence they came and wither they go.

—Ramsey Clark

1
Money

A retired husband is often a wife's full-time job.

—Ella Harris

Whine A: Where did it go?

Why: Money is an issue of note at all stages of life, but it takes on exaggerated importance to seniors, for whom twilight years can easily slip into the Twilight Zone without the security of a proper nest egg. Even with a solid retirement plan, seniors are likely to see a drop in their income that will force them to scrape their pennies together and send them into paroxysms of whining. The problem is that all the fun things cost extra, so that many seniors resign themselves to a life of bare minimums, and simply whine about everything they can't afford—or do anymore—to pass what time they have left.

Whine B: There's never enough.

Cure: The **"stop saving"** cure works for seniors because it's the perfect time of life to stop saving for a rainy day and start spending like it's pouring down in buckets. The goal here is to run out of money on the day you die, or better yet, the day after. This way there will be enough money to pay for your farewell festivities, which you will have (very festively) planned to the final detail on your deathbed while enjoying the pastry or cocktail that was bought with your last few carefully allotted dollars. *Bon Voyage.*

2
Aging

Whine A: I ache all over. I'm crippled.

Why: It is not fun to get old. No matter what anyone tries to tell you, it is a pain the butt...and the hips, and the shoulders and the neck and the hands and...well, you get the picture: The aches and pains that accompany the aging process are a fact of life. They are unavoidable and must be dealt with one way or another. On some days, just looking in the mirror and seeing some grumpy, old, unfamiliar person looking back at you can be devastating. The days I see my father's face in mine can be really rough for me.

Whine B: This isn't fun anymore.

Cure: The **"stop looking in the mirror"** cure works for seniors because it allows them to act any age they choose, even the age they remember as the best times of their lives. If you're 80 and that time was 40 years ago, then be 40 again. No one can dictate how you feel on the inside or control how you act on the outside. Remember, you are the star of your own show, so make it a good one! It is time to start doing things that amuse, amaze and astound you rather than continue a cycle of activities that only makes you kvetch and complain *ad nauseum*. Luckily, seniors don't have to impress anybody except themselves, unless they are unlucky enough to still be circulating in the dating world...

3
Loneliness

Whine A: Nobody cares about me.

Why: If you think aging is difficult, try doing it alone. Most seniors are alone through no fault of their own, as in widowhood. Many are just too devastated to even try to socialize. It's not easy for some seniors to make new friends or fresh starts. Of course, some older people prefer to be alone, especially if their past partners drove them crazy or were idiots. Also, loneliness is a very effective weapon for laying guilt trips on children. It can be lethally useful and extremely effective.

Whine B: No one ever calls me.

Cure: The **"find someone quick"** cure is the best approach for most seniors. It's not easy, but you have to get back in the game if you don't want your playing days to come to an abrupt end. These days you don't have to get married again. Many swinging seniors' lives are filled with all sorts of exciting events. Just don't tell your kids! Some things are best kept private, especially on the fast and fun freeways of freedom and frivolity.

4
Losing Things

To have a grievance is to have a purpose in life.

—*Alan Corey*

Whine A: Now where did I put it?

Why: Sadly, losing things is an everyday occurrence for most seniors. Somehow, things just have a way of disappearing. It is nature's cruel way of reminding us to try to remember where we put our stuff so that we won't altogether lose our already fading memories. For example, reading glasses are usually found on the top of your head. This malicious joke cannot really be considered practical since it is definitely impractical to spend most of your time looking for things you left on your head.

Whine B: I can't find it/them anywhere.

Cure: The **"reading glasses everywhere"** cure involves buying so many glasses—or so many of any other thing that you find you need all the time—that you can leave them at all of your checkpoints. This would mean at your bedside, at every phone in the house, at the computer, anywhere you read and in your purse or pocket. Oh yes, and don't forget the bathroom. As for all the other things you are constantly losing, such as keys, wallets, purses, hearing aids, grocery coupons, dentures and other such senior paraphernalia, good luck, and try not to lose your head even if you do occasionally misplace your teeth.

5
Forgetting Things

> **Women always worry about the things men forget;**
> **Men always worry about things women remember.**
>
> *—Daren Davenport*

Whine A: I can't remember anything!

Why: After a certain age, no matter who you are, you will start forgetting things. It starts with little things like forgetting where you parked the car or forgetting an appointment, or blanking on the name of someone you've known for ages. Somehow, the more concerned you become about forgetting, the more things you forget and the more often you forget them. It is a vicious cycle that sometimes pre-shadows dementia or the dreaded Alzheimer's disease. So whine while you can, seniors, if you must, for tomorrow you may forget to do so.

Whine B: Where did I leave it?

Cure: The **"write it down"** cure is the only one that seems to work in this situation. It means making lists and then trying very, very hard not to lose those lists so that you can refer to them later. My husband, Buckeye Leif, spends most of his time looking for his little red book. This frees him up from forgetting all the other things he needs to remember to forget. It is critical to never forget where you left your wife or husband. He or she is the very person who might remember where you put everything else.

6
Health

You know you're getting old when all the names
in your black book have **M.D.** after them.

—*Arnold Palmer*

Whine A: I'm not what I used to be.

Why: This is a common whine because it is so essential for enjoying life to be in good health. Seniors tend to overreact about their health issues, and that is understandable: Nobody likes being sick or feeling miserable. Unfortunately, it is just a cruel and immutable fact of life that old people get sick more often and more easily the older they become, and if that isn't cause for some good, old-fashioned whining, I don't know what is.

Whine B: I'm always sick and tired.

Cure: The **"denial"** cure is extreme, but it is your best chance to fool yourself and others into thinking you are healthy if you happen to be a senior on the wane. This means pushing yourself even when you don't feel like it. Putting on a good act can sometimes turn things around or at least postpone the inevitable. It helps to be a little crazy and to laugh a lot, especially at your self. If you work hard on this "everything's ship-shape" act, you should be able to provide plenty of eccentric tales for your eulogy. When I think of my own demise, I always try to remember that dying is easy, comedy is hard and writing a humorous eulogy is even harder.

7

Boredom

> Boredom is like a pitiless zooming in on the epidermis of time.
> Every instant is dilated and magnified like
> the pores of the face.
>
> —*Charlotte Whitton*

Whine A: There's nothing to do.

Why: It goes with the senior scene and ethos to have done most everything already. Nothing seems new and exciting anymore. It's hard to get energized about anything aside from a really good bowel movement. The "*carpe diem*" command loses its relevance and volitional force after a half a century of just trying to get through the day. Finding new and stimulating things to do is a challenge for everyone who's growing old (and I guess that would be just about everyone), but one that can be overcome if you stop whining and start doing something that has the power to take your mind off the boredom that sometimes engulfs you.

Whine B: I've done it already.

Cure: The **"roller coaster"** cure is my husband Buckeye's way of dealing with boredom. Instead of staying home bellyaching about being bored, off he goes to the amusement park to amuse himself. He is one of the few seniors around who has a year-round pass to Magic Mountain, but you must remember that the kind of magic this cure offers won't happen if you stay home just wishing for something fun and new to entertain you. Forget your age and go entertain yourself. Be a kid at heart if not in fact.

8
Retirement

The trouble with retirement is
that you never get a day off.

—*Abe Lemons*

Whine A: I have too much time on my hands.

Why: Some seniors love doing nothing while others hate being on the sidelines. Seniors can fill their time quite handily with low-impact sports and other leisure outings if they're still active enough to do so. But, for instance, how much golf can one man play? My husband found out during his own retirement, when his handicap went up four points because he was playing everyday. After only ten months of the "good life, Buckeye threw in the towel and went back to work. I didn't try to stop him. If you're not mobile enough to frolic and play, just sit still and do nothing and try to enjoy it. After a while, you'll realize that it's actually so pleasant to sit and do nothing that you'll wish you had more time to do just that. This revelation will occur just about when your time finally runs out.

Whine B: How did I ever have time to work?

Cure: The **"get a life, like start doing some volunteer work or something"** cure is what you need to combat senior boredom. You need to design your life around something other than the broadcast times of *Oprah* and *Ellen*. The best plan for combating boredom in your final years is to try to run out of steam rather than just simmering out.

9
Dying

Whine A: I wish I were dead.

Why: It is natural to worry about dying. It is a cruel joke on our species that we are the only ones who know for certain that we will die. Thus, the dying whine is extremely effective for getting attention. It is a great opportunity to lay a final guilt trip on those you deem worthy of such. It is hard to ignore this whine since it may come back and bite you. Actually it *will* come back, without question, and you won't know when, how or where. Seniors don't turn daft just because they're old and dying: Most of them know exactly what they're doing when using this whine, especially on their richly guilt-deserving children.

Whine B: I might as well be dead.

Cure: The **"so I might as well do whatever the hell I want"** cure will remedy this kind of whining. Since nobody cares about you or what happens to you anyway, why not do something that you have always wanted to do but have never done because of how it would affect others or reflect on you? Be naughty, pull pranks, drive too fast, say something racy to that young thing at the supermarket checkout counter next time you're there...anything that makes you feel like your doing exactly what you want to do no matter how trivial, and despite the fact that death is breathing down your neck.

10
Insomnia

**The best cure for insomnia
is knowing it's time to get up.**

—*Yana Packard*

Whine A: I can't fall asleep.

Why: Some seniors have a hard time sleeping due to anxiety attacks, which increase as one gets older. Since older folks tend to be early risers, you would think it would be easier for them to go to sleep at night, but bedtime can actually be the most difficult and worrisome time of the day for them. When you are running out of time, each moment left is part of the final countdown. It is hard to fall asleep when you feel like you are sitting in a space shuttle ready to launch with an unknown estimated time of departure: an ETD that could suddenly reveal itself as a certainty at any time of the day or night...

Whine B: I was up all night.

Cure: The **"Nighty night with Ambien"** cure is excellent for any senior struggling with insomnia. These are miracle pills that assist you in achieving a high quality, full night's sleep without a morning-after hangover. This medicine is not sold over the counter, so you will have to run this by your doctor. My experience is that Ambien is to women what Viagra is to men. Daily, Buckeye and I thank God for both and for each other.

Best Overall Remedy
for Whining Seniors

The Dying Without
Whining Cure

I actually started writing about whining when I wrote a book called *Dying without Whining.* I never published it because my mentor told me it was a lousy title for a book. The combination of the words dying and whining would attract only a small, select market composed of people who had terminal diseases, he warned me. Since it was meant to be a humorous tome, my small market might have skewed even smaller due to the fact that most people do not find humor in death, especially their own.

Now that I'm once again writing about whining, I want to share with you my original premise for the book: No matter who you are, the thought of dying can be frightening. Most of us don't believe it really will happen to us, foolishly hoping that we, of all people, will escape it in the end. Many of us are scared and tend to whine about our inevitable end. My theory will humorously put a positive spin on a negative topic.

To initiate this healing, try to think of all the things you will never have to do again once you are dead. I know this sounds morbid, but just give it a chance. You will be surprised at how long a list it will be. Things like standing in line, dealing with in-laws, and worrying about money are popular choices. You can also add dying to this list since it's also something you'll never have to do again once it's done.

Another thing you won't have to do anymore once you die is live. That's right, living just won't be the problem it once was anymore, and neither, you realize after some time compiling your list, will *anything* else.

Freed now as you have made yourself from worldly cares and the fear of death or living, you are ready to see your own earthly demise for what it actually may be: not the end of the tunnel but rather an incredible escape hatch. It could be the ultimate adventure, the supreme surprise party.

After you have recorded the things you will be relieved never to have to do again, then the fun part begins. You may now write down what you will do instead. The things you really want to do. The things you want to do right away. All of the things you have not done or put off for various reasons will flood into the channels of your mind. By writing them down, you will own them and they will become your reality.

This adventure will help you to stop the negative flow of energy in and out of your life and replace it with a positive one. Hopefully you will release the child within, allowing yourself the freedom to be a silly, funny, outrageous person. Suddenly, the wacky things that you have only dreamt about will become possibilities.

As an example, my husband Buckeye is a pilot and has always lived his life with a checklist in the cockpit. It consists of everything he wants to do before his final departure to that great runway in the sky. You, too, can have such a checklist; and remember, it doesn't always have to be about you.

My husband even helped our 86-year-old brother-in-law finish up his own list. They went off on an adventure to Brussels so that he could find his girlfriend from WWII. This quest was a real leap of faith since our brother-in-law had not heard from the girlfriend since the war. He knew her name and what town she lived in. So what more would you need to know? When it comes to impossible dreams, this was a big one. The good news was that they found her. The bad news was that her memory wasn't very good, and she didn't quite recognize her old love. No matter, it was all about the quest and the new memory Buckeye and his brother were creating together.

The goal here is to truly live each day as if it were your last day. The objective is to let go and do everything you can that will fill your life with love and laughter. It is time to take care of your unfinished business. It is okay to get angry and let it all out. No one will ever have to see this private list except you. More importantly, it is time for you to get off the treadmill and start enjoying this wonderful amusement park called life.

The best part is that you don't have to pretend to be nice anymore. Say what you think. Do what you want. It's your life and nobody's business except yours. This cure is especially effective after you're sixty. Then you can get away with anything because most people, especially your children, will think it's early dementia. They'll either agree with you to shut you up or ignore you. It's a win-win-win situation for you or that special brother-in-law.

Chapter Eight

Women

Women were born to whine. It is in their DNA. Women get introduced to whining by their mothers from the moment they are born in the delivery room. The little drama queens continue when they get home and perfect their craft throughout their lives. Whining starts out earlier with little girls than little boys because, while most men want to dominate, women always want to communicate more than anything no matter what age they are.

Did you know that women speak over 7,000 words a day and men speak only 2,000 words? Now just who do you think can get in more whining time? It's a hard job but someone has got to do it. Whining and shoes are to women what sports and Home Depot are to men.

Whining about not losing weight or having a bad hair day is just the tip of the iceberg for most women. Our biggest whine these days is, or should be, "Please, please stop the war and the killing." Women know that the only arms we need are those we use for hugging.

> **The thing women have yet to learn is *nobody*
> gives you power. You just take it.**
>
> —*Roseanne Barr*

Top Ten
Women's Whines

#1 Weight
#2 Bad Hair Days
#3 Family
#4 Clothes
#5 Aging
#6 Cell Phones
#7 Flying
#8 Exhaustion
#9 Wars
#10 Gynecologists

Women who seek to be equal with men lack ambition.

—Timothy Leary

1
Weight

Whine A: I'm so fat.

Why: Weight is by far the biggest whine of women everywhere, and it's easy to see why: Our culture and media have made ultra-thin the gender standard by portraying stick-skinny celebrities as the only ones who truly have it all. Many women think that if they could only lose some weight, even their most chronic problems would disappear. This is patently untrue. Their weight problems will disappear, yes, but others may be magnified if they don't go "poof" immediately, as planned. I've been both light and heavy. Sure, I like being light better, but even if thin is "in," it won't make you happy.

Whine B: I can't lose weight.

Cure: I recommend the **"break the diet addiction"** cure for women who whine about weight, and I do so from personal experience. I have been on one diet or another for half of my life. I'm still looking for that magic pill. But I know the only way I can stay really healthy and fit is to simply eat a balanced, nutrient-rich diet of fresh foods. The reason it's so difficult to break the diet addiction is that it's scary to be responsible for your own figure and health, and so much easier to put your trust in a guru or pill that tells you what it's going to do to you, even if it doesn't come through. This cure puts you in charge of your own body, and through it, your destiny: powerful juju, ladies!

2
Bad Hair Days

Women go to beauty parlors
for the un-mussed look men hate.

—*Mignon McLaughlin*

Whine A: My hair's a mess.

Why: The truth is that hairdressers created the myth about a woman's hair being her crowning glory. That being said, a bad hair day can really screw things up when you are just trying to get through your already trying routine. If your hair is a mess and you can't do anything with it, you feel like a failure in every area of your life. Your hair affects your mood and your mood affects everyone who is within whining distance.

Whine B: I can't do anything with it.

Cure: The **"find a good hairdresser"** cure is the solution to your bad hair day drama. And once you have found him or her, never, never ever, let those magic clippers go. I have been with my hairdresser Paul for over thirty years now. When I lived in London, I actually flew home to L.A. once a month to get my hair done. I pretended I was coming home to tend to the family business. The truth is that my hairdresser is also my therapist. He knows all my secrets. He's so good that now my daughters go to him to find out how to handle me.

3
Families

👤 👤 👤 👤　👤 👤 👤 👤 👤　👤 👤 👤 👤

> **Despite their families and their families' families,**
> **most families are as bad as anyone else's families.**
>
> —*January Jones*

Whine A: They're driving me crazy.

Why: Women whine about their families because they can and it feels good. Families provide great material for compulsive whiners. Whether it is your parents, siblings, spouses, kids or in-laws, there is always something they do that can drive you crazy. Whining about family usually doesn't really do a whole lot of good, but it will empower you so that you think you are doing something. It is amazing how people you love so much can become the same people you love to hate.

Whine B: I can't stand them.

Cure: The **"ignore them"** cure is one that will let *you* drive *them* crazy for a change. Instead of whining or complaining about your family to anyone who will listen, try pretending they don't even exist. This is a hard one to pull off, especially if you see them all the time. If you can actually rise above the fray, it will allow you to see them from a fresh perspective. This cure can backfire if none of them realizes that they are being ignored, and it is definitely time to stop treatment if they begin to show actual signs of happiness about being ignored.

4
Clothes & Shoes

Shopping for bathing suits is worse than taking your mother-in-law to lunch.

—*Anonymous Daughter-in-Law*

Whine A: I can't find anything I like.

Why: The wardrobe issue is tricky for any woman. Your husband thinks you have too many things while you know you don't have enough. Clothes and shoes can become real addictions for many women because buying them makes us feel wonderful. With styles and trends changing every day, it is not easy to keep up or even keep even. Just when you think you have enough clothes for any occasion— or does any woman ever think that?—you find that you must buy something new for a special event. And when you go out shopping for it, you can't find a thing. Of course, when you're just browsing, you love everything, which leads you to buy tons of garments you don't really need or want to wear.

Whine B: Nothing looks good on me.

Cure: The **"shop till you drop"** cure works for me. Nothing can make you feel better about yourself than a great, well-tailored outfit or a fantastic, sexy new pair of shoes. Women must be designed to receive an immediate rush of adrenaline upon finding the right thing for an affordable price. Then there are the times you can't afford it but buy it anyway. I even know of a few women who are sneak shoppers, and hide their extravagant purchases from their husbands under their beds.

5
Aging

> **Every girl should use what Mother Nature gave her before Father Time takes it away.**
>
> *—Laurence J. Peter*

Whine A: I'm getting old.

Why: Whining about aging has been going on ever since Eve looked at her reflection in the golden pond of Eden. Aging reminds us of our mortality. It can be very depressing, especially if your life on earth as a human is not going well, which hardship always reflects itself in the wrinkles and natural expressions of the face. There are no miracle creams or potions that can make you feel better about aging. The myth that you're not getting older but getting better is just something old folks created to make themselves feel better about getting older.

Whine B: I look like a prune.

Cure: The **"break the mirrors"** cure came to me from one of my survey participants. She wisely suggested that if I felt old to just stop looking in mirrors. Since I have no willpower, I think it would be easier to break all the mirrors. If you are superstitious and want to avoid seven years of bad luck, you can just remove all the mirrors from the premises. Think of how easy life would be without mirrors. No need to comb you hair or check your lipstick. No more wrinkles, no lumps, no sags and especially, no bags.

6
Cell Phones

👤 👤 👤 👤 👤 👤 👤 👤 👤 👤 👤 👤

> **I drive with my knees. Otherwise, how can I put on my lipstick and talk on my phone?**
>
> —*Sharon Stone*

Whine A: I can't find it.

Why: When I first got my cell phone, I thought it was something I would never use but conceded to my loved ones that it might be a good idea in case of an emergency. Little did I know that my cell phone would become my one consistent lifeline to my family and friends. When I accidentally misplace it, which is more often than I would ever admit, I automatically launch into an intense whine, the urgent tones of which I never hear myself use otherwise. If the sound is turned off on the little bugger, I can't even call myself to find out where I left it, which really drives me insane.

Whine B: Do you know where it is?

Cure: The **"never turn it off"** cure will solve the lost cell phone mystery. This way you can always find it, even under the car seat or out by the jacuzzi. It can be somewhat valid to whine about lost cell phones since they have practically become almost limb-like appendages for many humans. Without one, we feel lost and forsaken. I plug mine into the charger faithfully every night unless I have lost it. Then I go nuts trying to find it, looking everywhere—even in the refrigerator. As for the wicked and the weary, there is no rest for the cell phone loser.

7
Flying

> I feel about airplanes the way I feel about diets.
> It seems to me that they are wonderful things
> for other people to go on.
>
> —*Jean Kerr*

Whine A: I hate flying.

Why: I whine about flying because my first husband died in an airplane crash—I get a free pass on this one. The reality is that most women whine about flying because it scares them silly. Also, hurtling to the ground in a twisted hunk of flaming metal at lightning speeds just doesn't sound like a very pleasant way to die. Women are smart and pragmatically oriented enough to know that flying is statistically safer than driving. But let me ask you, who can be pragmatic when one's life is on the line?

Whine B: How does this thing stay up?

Cure: The **"get mildly drunk"** cure will guarantee that you will conquer your fear of flying. You don't need to get horribly drunk, just enough so you can quietly pass out during the flight. This is called "bottle courage," and it can also come in other forms such as sleeping pills or very strong anti-depressants. You may wake up with a hangover but you will be alive. The best part is that you will have no memory of your on-board torture, though your hair and makeup might need a little refreshing.

8
Exhaustion

Whine A: I'm beat.

Why: For women, whining about being tired or exhausted is as common as breathing. This is especially true of young mothers in two-income households. They put in a full day of work at the office, and then they come home to their really, *really* big job, raising a family. There just aren't enough hours in the day for anyone to work two jobs fulltime. With the constantly rising cost of living outstripping income raises coast to coast, this is a way of life too many women both young and old are forced to embrace.

Whine B: I'm so tired I can't move.

Cure: The **"pace yourself"** cure is the best way to tackle your exhaustion. Try to slow down and do one thing at a time. Multi-tasking takes its toll. Remember that sharing your daily load of work will only work if *you* make it work. Some chores at home can and should wait until your husband does them. Another approach is to turn this system inside out and include sleeping as a chore that needs to be shared between you and your spouse. Remember, it is important to smell the roses while taking the rubbish out. Also, it's okay to make the bed while you're still in it.

9
Wars

Most men want to dominate,
while most women would rather communicate.

—*Mari Jonassen*

Whine A: Why is this going on?

Why: It is my belief that wars are created to make rich men richer. No one can argue that big bucks are made during every war, and only ever by a select few. The reality is that all wars are basically civil wars since we are all children of God. Women whine about ending wars because sending our children off to die is something that is unacceptable. It is a difficult reality to comprehend, and will never make sense to any mother or grandmother. Perhaps this is because fathers and grandfathers are the ones who send young men off to fight their wars.

Whine B: How can we stop it?

Cure: The **"stop the war"** cure for women is what I propose for this specific whining malady. This would revolve around supporting the troops while standing up to people who are using our children to wage wars that cannot be won. Be informed, try talking and listening to some Vietnam veterans. I have walked behind a flag-draped coffin and know the pain of losing a husband. I can't even begin to imagine what it must be like to lose a child. I try not to get too political, but some things, whether you agree or not, have to be said. So say it, already—you'll feel better!

10
The Gynecologist

♀ ♀ ♀ ♀ ♀ ♀ ♀ ♀ ♀ ♀ ♀ ♀

> A male gynecologist is like an auto mechanic
> who has never owned a car.
>
> —*Carrie Snow*

Whine A: I hate going.

Why: Going to the gynecologist is something every woman hates. It is just no fun to be examined in such an intimate place in such an intimate way. This procedure can be particularly unpleasant when you are using a male gynecologist. I know this sounds very sexist, but having talked to hundreds on the subject over the years, I can safely say that it is the way most women feel. As for a mammogram, it hurts and it's cold. Let's put it this way: Anything else would be better—even going to the dentist. Then again, childbirth trumps them all.

Whine B: I really, really hate going.

Cure: The **"pick a woman doctor"** cure helps in overcoming this whine. Again, at the risk of sounding like the sexist that I am on this topic, it is so much easier doing this examination with a woman. It just feels better. Knowing that she has to go through this also somehow makes it more tolerable. It helps to have someone who is simpatico when taking your smear or smashing your boobs.

Best Overall Cure
for Whining Women

The Get Over Jackie Kennedy Cure

Did you know that women speak over 7,000 words a day and men speak only 2,000 words? I'm always amazed at this statistic. Can you guess who might be doing most of the whining? See, I'm not really that sexist after all!

I think that women from my generation owe a lot of their misery and whining to Jackie Kennedy. She was a magnificent first lady whom we admired and tried to emulate. Unfortunately for most of us, she was an idol that none of us could touch. She lived the fantasy life that we could only dream about. Even her tragedies were magnificent. She not only married two of the most powerful men in the world, but she was also a world-class shopper. She wrote the book when it came to spending a husband's money.

In order to get over your womanly whining for once and for all, you have to get over Jackie and start thinking in terms of real women; women such as Eleanor, Condoleezza and Hillary. You may not agree with their politics, but you'll agree that their intelligence far exceeds their beauty. We need to identify with real women, like us, instead of fantasy princesses, in order to become real ourselves.

Chapter Nine

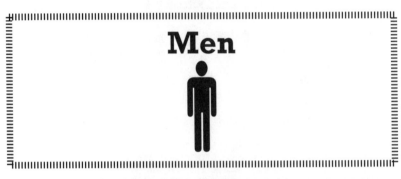

Men

All men no matter what their age whine about the same things. Can you imagine a world without men? There would be no Power Rangers, no wrestling, no wars and no ESPN. It used to be that he who made the gold made the rules. But now it seems to be that he who makes the gold rules the remote.

When it comes to sports whining, it's not whether you win the big game or lose it, but rather who to blame. My husband can whine whether his team wins or loses. If they win, then it's not by enough. If they lose, especially a national championship, "How can that be?" It doesn't help that he's an Ohio State Buckeye, the consistently second best team in the country.

Whining is difficult for most men because it reminds them of the dreaded "F" word of relationships, and I'm not talking about what you think I'm talking about. There's not a man alive who wouldn't rather talk about sports than their **F**eelings. The reality of life is that if it has tires or testicles, you're going to have trouble with it.

> **Can you imagine a world without men?**
> **No crime, no wars and no ESPN.**
>
> —*January Jones*

Top Ten
Men's Whines

#1   Money

#2   Jobs and Bosses

#3   Losing Teams

#4   Taxes and Politics

#5   Cable TV

#6   Aging and Fitness

#7   Going Shopping

#8   Gas Prices

#9   Wives and Kids

#10 Mother-in-Laws

It's a man's world,
and you men can have it.

—*Katherine Anne Porter*

1
Money

👤 👤 👤 👤 👤 👤 👤 👤 👤 👤 👤 👤

> Money isn't everything,
> but it's a long way ahead of what comes next.
>
> —*Edmund Stockdale*

Whine A: There's never enough.

Why: It is hard to keep ahead of inflation along with the daily cost of living. Traditionally the family's financial stability has been the man's responsibility. As for today's modern male, despite his possibly gender-equal leanings, the attachment he still displays to his role as head of the household is something he has inherited from a long line of men who didn't have wives out in the work force. And now that we're there along with them, we know there's no end of whining to do about the burden of making a living.

Whine B: Interest payments are all I can do.

Cure: The **"two income household"** cure makes a big difference in the outlook of men who are trying to make good financial decisions for their families. Unfortunately, working women can't be in two places at once, so their children pay the price. There is no easy solution besides a commitment to job-sharing when raising children. On the other hand, money is not such a big problem for men who choose to remain single. They are easy to recognize. They always look happy, as if they don't have a care in the world. Their only concern is who's going to win The Super Bowl.

2
Jobs and Bosses

> **Nothing is really work unless you would rather be doing something else.**
>
> —*James Matthew Barrie*

Whine A: I work so hard for so little.

Why: All men dream of having a job that will allow them to do something they love while getting paid big bucks. They also dream about having a great, fun-loving boss who carries on like Bill Clinton in the oval office. Unfortunately for them, this seldom happens. Most men struggle with jobs that they feel trapped in along with bosses who are idiots. Once they are working in a job with all sorts of responsibilities, it is hard to make a change. Inertia overtakes them, and then they then have to settle or self destruct, the former of which is far cleaner and less harmful to others, though they may not feel so spotless themselves for having made such a compromise.

Whine B: They take me for granted.

Cure: The **"dream job"** cure deals with jobs and bosses that are a pain. Right from the get go, try to land a job that you love doing. Sometimes you can even find a boss you like. The best way to find the ideal job is to follow your passion. Find the thing that you love doing the most, and then do it. If you aren't there yet, keep trying. It's not easy, but if you succeed, your wife, children and your dog will thank you for all sorts of benefits that will trickle down to them from your own elevated mood and lack of workplace whining.

3
Losing Sports Teams

> It's hard to win a pennant,
> but it's harder to lose one.
>
> —*Chuck Tanner*

Whine A: How could they lose?

Why: Many men live solely to cheer on and support their favorite teams. During the season, they all become fanatics. They are unbelievably loyal to their college or hometown teams. Each year, they know that this is the year they'll win the championship. My husband, Buckeye Leif, is an Ohio State fan and...need I say more? He lives, breathes and dies for Ohio State. It is amazing that he was even able to marry me since I was born in Michigan. His favorite cheer is *Muck Fichigan!*

Whine B: We need a new coach.

Cure: The **"next season"** cure is the only satisfactorily hopeful answer after a losing season. During the off-season, men can escape from reality by dreaming about winning the championship next year. My husband lives for the day the rankings come out. It is the biggest day of the year for him. When I said "for better or worse," I didn't know we were taking vows that included the entire Ohio State football team, the consistently second best team in the country.

4
Taxes and Politics

> They say women talk too much.
> If you worked in Congress,
> you'd know that the filibuster was invented by men.
>
> —*Clare Booth Luce*
>
> America is a land of taxation
> that was founded to avoid taxation.
>
> —*Laurence J. Peters*

Whine A: They're all bastards.

Why: Men adore complaining about taxes and politics because they can. They know that, aside from running for political office, there really isn't much they can do but complain. They need something to complain about when they don't want to think about their team losing the big game. After sports, taxes and politics are the topics that men feel they know the most about.

Whine B: They're all crooks.

Cure: The **"forget it"** cure will remind men that it is pointless to whine about things they can't fix. It is more important to whine about the things that really matter—things they can do something about, like cheering for their favorite football teams or, if they live in Boston, their favorite baseball team. If that doesn't work for them, then they can watch The Golf Channel.

5
Cable TV

> **Today, watching television often means fighting, violence and foul language—and that's just deciding who gets to hold the remote control.**
>
> —*Donna Gephart*

Whine A: Oh, No! Not now!

Why: The worst day in Buckeye's life was when our cable TV went out during the last few seconds of a close Ohio State vs. Michigan football game. It was not a total disaster since he was able to quickly call long distance back to Ohio to get a play-by-play from his niece and nephew. Now, this is a man who can handle a crisis situation with ingenuity and quick wits, both of which come in handy in his twin careers: piloting airplanes and rooting for the Buckeyes.

Whine B: I've had it.

Cure: The **"TiVo"** cure makes sure that men can digitally record all the sporting events that they just can't miss—and play them back without commercials. Not only will they be happier not to be interrupted by ads, but watching the game will also take less time away from time they could be spending with their wives and/or families. This cure works especially well when a man wants to keep watching his team win over and over again. As for losses, those can easily be deleted and forgotten with one click of the remote. Remotes are to men what shoes are to women. These are two things that neither sex, respectively, can live without.

6
Aging and Fitness

> **Health nuts are going to feel stupid someday lying in hospitals dying of nothing.**
>
> *—Redd Foxx*

Whine A: Getting old sucks.

Why: Men hate getting older as much as, if not more than, women. The reason is that aging interferes with their fantasy lives as jocks. Most men never lose the desire to play ball, even when they sit behind a desk five days a week. Take my husband as an example: Buckeye plays on a senior's baseball team and a tennis team, and then plays golf with his buddies. A good day for him is a four-sport day. It begins with sex in the morning, senior baseball mid-morning, then league tennis at noon and golf to finish up the day. This obsession with playing sports, along with sex, is something that men never outgrow, and any challenge to this obsession reveals rich soil for the cultivation of the fine and underrated art of male whining.

Whine B: I'm not getting any younger.

Cure: The **"play ball"** cure is the one I believe works the best. Why fight it? Men never lose their desire to compete. This is a good thing health-wise because everyone knows that if you don't use it you will lose it. Men might as well use their vital energy and drive to compete like little hellions on the ball field as turn it toward dieting or sticking to a strict exercise regimen. Obvious benefits will ensue in the aging and fitness arenas; and as most women know, this cure does not only refer to sports.

7
Going Shopping

Whine A: Do I have to go?

Why: In general, men hate shopping for anything unless it is related to their sports "career." Getting my husband to go shopping anywhere but Home Depot is next to impossible. He won't even shop for his own clothes. Because of this, he is a prime target for the fashion police, but he would rather go to the dentist than shop for clothes. If I want to take him anywhere on a trip, I not only have to shop for his traveling clothes, but then must tell him what to wear day by day. Fortunately, he likes my taste.

Whine B: Can't we go tomorrow?

Cure: The **"don't complain"** cure is for men who don't like to go shopping and then don't like what you buy. If my husband ever complains, which he seldom does, I answer with the classic, "If you don't like it, you can do it yourself." This is my all-occasion reply for most things that men complain about. As for the money spent on his wardrobe, it is worthless to him if it doesn't go towards clothes and equipment that might improve the look, feel, potential or potency of his grand athletic endeavors.

8
Gas Prices

♟ ♟ ♟ ♟   ♟ ♟ ♟ ♟   ♟ ♟ ♟ ♟

It's cheaper to buy beer than gasoline.

—*Leif Jonassen, III*

Whine A: This is ridiculous.

Why: It's true, the price of gasoline is ridiculous and getting more so by the minute. The problem with men is that they take it personally. They feel manipulated by the gas companies and the powers that be in Washington, and they're especially perturbed when gas prices are so blatantly manipulated around election time every year. Gas prices are particularly frustrating to men because their cars are their prized possessions. Some men would live in their cars if they could, even if they couldn't afford the gas to drive them.

Whine B: What are they charging today?

Cure: The **"buy a hybrid"** cure is not only a statement against gas prices, but it also helps to save the environment. This is a feel-good cure because ownership of a hybrid makes men feel they are making a statement and fighting back against the gas companies. A man can easily fantasize that he is "The Man of La Mancha" fighting the impossible fight! Even though they won't win, this is far preferable to fighting with their wives.

9
Wives and Kids

↑ ↑ ↑ ↑ ↑ ↑ ↑ ↑ ↑ ↑ ↑ ↑

> My theory is that men
> are no more liberated than women.
>
> —*Indira Gandhi*

Whine A: *Give me a break.*

Why: Men whine about their wives and children because, frankly, they are easier to whine about than a losing football team. They are close by, thus convenient targets for whining. In addition, men get a lot of sympathy and understanding from other men when they whine about their wives and kids—perfect targets for a good ol' poker-night man-whine. Wives are really good targets for whining anywhere, in fact, any time; kids don't become good targets until they are teenagers who constantly demand to drive your car.

Whine B: *Cut me some slack.*

Cure: The **"good times"** cure was created to remind men to remember how they felt about their wives and children when they met. Your wife was all of your fantasies come true. Your children were adorable at birth—well, maybe not in the delivery room, but after they were cleaned up in the nursery, they became shining little embodiments of all your hopes and dreams, and you couldn't thank your wife enough for bestowing them upon the two of you. These are the memories you need to cling to as time goes by. If successful, you will find your desire to whine about your wife and kids steadily fading away as you start to fade away, grow old and lose your memory.

10
Mothers-in-Law

> **Defining the proper punishment for bigamy:**
> **Two mother-in-laws.**
>
> —*Lord John Russell*

Whine A: Oh no, it's her again!

Why: Mother-in-laws are the bane of most men's existences because they think that no one is good enough for their precious daughters. This makes them a natural enemy of all married men. Occasionally this syndrome will be broken when a mother-in-law is available as a gratis babysitter. Until grandchildren are in the picture, this precarious relationship is pretty much of a stand-off, which is fine as long as both parties eventually understand that the bond must endure no matter how painful to its adherents.

Whine B: What did I do to deserve her?

Cure: The **"try to get along"** cure is a viable, if not easily applicable, solution. After all, supposedly you both love the same person—her daughter, who happens to be your wife. You need to remember that unless you put on a really good act, there will be no free childcare. Conversely, I have encountered isolated cases of true love and adoration between men and their wives' mothers. It doesn't happen too often, but like all miracles, it could happen and very infrequently does.

Best Overall Remedy
for Whining Men

The Sports Talk Cure

I created this cure with men in mind, but it will work just as well for anyone whose DNA is encrypted with a love of sports. No matter what the complaint may be, if you can change the subject to a sports question or observation, all whining will cease. Men, and especially boys, can easily be distracted by anything relating to their favorite game or team. Sports talk can transport them to their fantasy world, where they are superstars and their teams always win.

Unfortunately, this can backfire if they have just suffered a big loss. Anytime this happens, they are vulnerable to intense whining in order to relieve the pain. Is it something about the thrill of victory versus the agony of defeat? It doesn't matter whether it is a pick-up game on a sandlot or the World Series—the pain of losing is always unbearable for most men. After a big loss, it is best to just let men be alone or with other men who are losers too.

Once they have recovered, which depends on the severity of their loss, they will bounce right back to get ready for the next season. The nice thing about the sports talk cure is that you will never run out of material with which to bewitch whining men.

Chapter Ten

Best Friends

Friendship isn't one thing; it's a million little things.

Your best friends are the ones you have on speed dial. It's easy to identify them because they are the ones who make you feel good no matter how bad you think you feel. When you need someone at three in the morning, your best friend will take your call.

Best friends are the ones who will tell you the truth but not in a brutal way. They are the ones you invite to your pity party and the only present they bring is their presence in your life. When you whine with them, it's more like wining and dining.

Best friends are the ones who not only will help you bury the body after you murder your husband, but promptly forget where your buried it, as well. They will also never tell you that you need to lose weight or that your kids are spoiled rotten—unless you ask them to.

Friendship is an endless rosary of shared concerns and feelings to count together—yes, but best friends are also one solid thing: a copasetic union of trust and love that is stronger and more impressive than the sum of its parts. It is only because of this extreme solidarity that best friends can whine with abandon about anything at all to their hearts' content in each other's company.

> **A friend can tell you things
> you don't want to tell yourself.**
>
> —*Frances Ward*

Top Ten
Best Friends' Whines

#1 Weight

#2 Spouses

#3 Other People

#4 Social Life

#5 Children

#6 Holidays

#7 Supermarkets and Cooking

#8 Work Load

#9 PMS and Health

#10 Class Reunions

Best friends secretly worship together
at the Altar of Ambien, with a Belief in Botox,
along with the Love of Lipo!

—*The LOLAS*
The (lovely) Ladies of Las Amigas,
National Charity League
Conejo Chapter

1
Weight

It's okay to be fat. So you're fat.
Just be fat and shut up about it.

—*Roseanne Barr*

Whine A: I'm too fat.

Why: Your best friends are the only people you can whine to about your weight. They will understand, telling you what you need—or want—to hear, depending on your mood. Best friends are unconditional. If you need the brutal truth, they will do it a loving way. Sometimes you don't need the truth *per se*, but only someone to listen and respond with honesty. A best friend is someone who will tell you that you always look great to them and mean it, and then be able to turn around in the next breath and tell you exactly how many pounds you need to lose to look the way you think you want to look.

Whine B: I really tried, but I've gained again!

Cure: The **"buddy system"** cure will help both of you. What better way to lose weight than as the dynamic, drastic duo! The buddy system works particularly well when you and your best friend join a weight loss program or gym together. It's a great excuse to spend more time with your comrade in arms—the kind you use for hugging. I suggest going to a gym/spa that includes a massage and facial as part of the monthly fee. Even if you don't lose weight, you'll love the treatments. Then you can skip the workouts and still get your money's worth.

2

Spouses

> **If it has tires or testicles,**
> **you're going to have trouble with it.**
>
> *—January Jones*

Whine A: We always do what he wants.

Why: We whine to our best friends about our spouses because we need to get certain things off our chests about the way our partners treat, mistreat, adore and ignore us. When you are complaining to your best friend, you know your divulgences will remain strictly between the two of you. A best friend can be a safe haven on the stormy seas of matrimony, providing necessary emotional ballast during both squalls and doldrums. Nothing you can tell your best friends will shock them or make them think less of you. No matter what you say or do, your best friend will back you up whenever needed no matter what her own feelings. Of course, when she needs the spotlight, you turn it upon her immediately....

Whine B: He/she is driving me crazy.

Cure: The **"tell all"** cure helps to get things out into the open in a safe place where a secret can remain just that. Whining about anything with someone who is discrete goes a long way. It's like going to therapy with a therapist who will always take your side. Whatever you may have done, you were just having a bad day. Stuff happens, your best friend knows it and she will never harshly judge you for it. She will only harshly judge your husband or boyfriend.

3
Other Friends

Whine A: She never calls me.

Why: Some people have a hard time telling the difference between best friends, everyday friends and mere acquaintances. It takes time to find out whom you can really trust or who really cares about you in the way a family member might, if your family doesn't happen to be totally dysfunctional like most. It is hard to have more than one best friend at a time. I guess it happens to more than a few lucky people, but I've only seen it happen to old people in the old folks' home. They're the ones who can't remember who they are, let alone who their best friend might be, that day.

Whine B: She never listens to my problems.

Cure: The **"taker or giver"** cure will help you to see people as they really are, if you're willing to look. When friends let you down, that is the time to decide whether they are takers or givers. It's easy to identify them. The takers are the ones who make you tired. The givers are the ones who make you feel great. It is my Yin and Yang theory of friendship evaluation. When you need someone quick at 3:00 am, the Yins will take your call. The Yangs will tell you to leave a message, and they'll get back to you ASAP.

4
Social Life

> Some people go to priests;
> others to poetry; I to my friends.
>
> —*Virginia Woolf*

Whine A: What social life?

Why: Sometimes people whine to their best friends about getting in a rut together. You know the same people, go to the same places, and you tend to do the same boring things day in and day out. This is the path of least resistance, which leads to eventual stasis and malaise. By not doing anything different, you don't have to take the risk of being original. Being original and authentic with your best friend is actually important for the health of your relationship. Being the real thing, whatever that means to you, is a daunting challenge because it can be revealing or revolting to others, but at least it's...real!

Whine B: We never go out.

Cure: The **"let's be silly"** cure is what my best friends and I do when one of us is in the dumps. When life is over- or underwhelming, it takes friends to remind you that you can keep an even keel by remembering to be silly every once in a while. The Three Amigas, Susan, Yana and I, meet every Wednesday morning at breakfast for our weekly, wacky dose of laughing or crying. It's our much needed and appreciated therapy. No one has as much fun as we silly three. Our glee often also affects Linda, our waitress, who gladly shares in our session between orders and coffee refills.

5
Children and Day Care

> It's the friends you can call up
> in the middle of the night that matter.
>
> —*Howarth Rowe*

Whine A: It never stops.

Why: My best friends and I whine to each other about our children. We know that our role is to let them do their own thing. But it sure helps to share our concerns and comfort each other. Nowadays, young women who are best friends often whine to each other about finding good day care for their kids. Now that they all have to work, day care is a big issue for them and an even bigger one for their checkbooks.

Whine B: It's hard to find good help.

Cure: The **"Granny the Nanny"** cure is the one that my daughters have used for their day care problems. It's an obvious answer as long as Granny is willing and able to help out without resentment—and especially without charge. I love doing it when I can, but not all grannies might feel the same. I know a certain number of mature women who would just as soon swing eighteen holes with grandpa in the blazing sun as swing the baby-boos at a shady park. If Granny is not amenable or unavailable, you can always turn to other family members—or you can kid swap and co-op with your best friend.

6
Holidays

> **Holidays turn tired people into exhausted people.**
>
> —*Brooke Gabbey*

Whine A: I hate this time of year.

Why: I have a dear friend who leaves her tree up all year, which puts her ahead of me every holiday season. Close friends are the ones who know how holidays can get out of control and can run to your aid if needed at a moment's notice. Best friends are the ones who can seriously help you stay the course through the sometimes daunting emotional and practical obstacles that always present themselves at this time of year. Of course, there's always a spirit of friendly competition that resides between best friends around the holidays, too. Whose pie is better, whose wrappings more shiny? As for me, I love doing my Christmas Village and the kids love visiting when it's up. I wonder if my friend would mind if I kept it up all year like she does her tree.

Whine B: I have to do everything.

Cure: The **"no present"** cure means skipping presents at Christmas, thus cleanly cutting out a major holiday hassle. The "in-exchange" plan would be to do bigger birthday gifts throughout the year. Another idea is to celebrate with the family at Thanksgiving. This way the holiday stress will be over before Christmas arrives. Or you can do what we did in the Navy and celebrate on July 25! This will allow you to buy your Christmas gifts on sale in the off-season, when stores aren't crowded.

7
Supermarkets and Cooking

Whine A: I hate going to the supermarket.

Why: Everyone whines about having to go to the   supermarket. Best friends whine about it because it's the ultimate "been there, done that" experience. In Southern California, the only time I've seen women enjoy shopping was when Tom Selleck was spotted perusing lettuce at the local Gelsons. As the word spread, every shopping cart in the store began heading to the produce section.

Whine B: I hate cooking.

Cure: The **"go to Whole Foods"** cure is my favorite way to handle food shopping, cooking and cleaning up. Whole Foods is always a shopping delight. Everything is healthy, organic and makes you feel like a better person. The store's food court is to die for, offering fresh, hot, raw and/or organic omnivorous or vegetarian delicacies that require no cooking or cleaning up. I haven't seen Tom Selleck there yet, but it's a fun place for best friends to stake out just in case he shows up. Better yet, I interviewed Curtis Stone, *The Take Home Chef* on TLC, and he reports that he's at Whole Foods picking up ladies to cook with all the time, especially if you're young and cute.

8
Work Load

Anybody can face a crisis,
it's the day to day living that wears you out.

—*Anton Chekhov*

Whine A: They expect too much of me.

Why: We can all allow ourselves to get programmed to do too much for others while not being valued enough by anyone. You want recognition, but not at the expense of your dignity or integrity. If you are even reading this page, you are probably an "A" type and understand exactly what I'm talking about. A brief moment to whine about the day's triumphs and humiliations alike with your best friend can help you keep your head above the waters when they start to churn. Taking time to smell the flowers is a lovely thought, too, but extremely hard to manage while carrying a work load as heavy as you do—unless you accidentally trip into a flower bed on your day off.

Whine B: I'm taken for granted.

Cure: The **"drunch"** cure involves combining lunch with drinks that could make you so drunk that you wouldn't be able to tell the difference between brunch or lunch even if you cared. This cure means stopping whatever you're doing, calling your best friend and inviting her to take a break too. If she can't do lunch, then skip the "unch" and just do the "dr" Part. Our drunches usually consist of drinking our lunch with our other best friend, Bloody Mary, who has recently become a Virgin Mary for reasons I won't go into here.

9
PMS & Health

Women complain about premenstrual syndrome, but I think of it as the only time of month that I can be myself.

—*Roseanne*

Whine A: It's that time again.

Why: All best friends know this whine very well. They have been doing it since they were in their teens, and it has never changed since. You have supported each other through decades of bloating and irritability, but the real fun part of a woman's life cycle starts with peri-menopause, which brings on the hot sweats followed by the cold chills. One minute you're fine, and then, without warning, you are drowning in your own body fluids. The only good thing to say about menopause is that if you survive it without committing murder or mayhem, you will no longer have to endure monthly menses. Period!

Whine B: I've got cramps.

Cure: The **"hot or cold shower"** cure has helped me deal gracefully with both PMS and menopause. It seems suspiciously simple, but no matter what my body temperature was, I would jump into the shower to re-adjust it—and it would work wonders. The only problem with this cure is that you can start looking like a water-logged prune after only a few treatments. Also, you need to be able to shower in the dark. Then you don't have to look at yourself when you get out. Not pretty!

10
Class Reunions

It takes a long time to grow an old friend.

—*John Leonard*

Whine A: Should I go?

Why: As only best friends know, class reunions can be perilous. This is especially so if you haven't been to one in forty years. I must confess I was nervous. It had been too long. What would it be like seeing all my young best friends resurface as old women? I prayed there would be name tags with vintage pictures and very big printing. Luckily, my prayers were answered. The pictures were of 18-year-olds I couldn't begin to remember or recognize, but I could read the names. We all pretended that no one had changed. Ha, Ha!

Whine B: I really need to lose some weight.

Cure: The **"go for it"** cure is my reply to anyone on the fence about a reunion. We laughed together. We sang our school song and danced as only girls in all-girl Catholic schools know how to do. We hugged and cried remembering our friends who died. There was a rose for each of them, all sixteen. Nothing had changed; we were young again. Nobody ever forgets the fun of driving nuns crazy. The memories of our times shared together will remain in our hearts forever, though I can't say how soon we'll be kicking up our heels to dance on the same floor again. Soon, I hope!

The Pity Party Cure

> A lot of people want to ride with you in the limo, but
> what you want is someone who will take the bus
> with you when the limo breaks down.
>
> —*Oprah Winfrey*

My Mother had a cure for whining that she used on me, and it's one that I have successfully used on my own kids. It's similar to the Norwegian Ris-pa-rumpin Cure but not nearly as charming. Basically, it's another question approach with consequences. The question is always asked in a mother's "I mean business" tone of voice, and it goes like this: "If you want to whine, do you want me to give you something to *really* whine about right now?" It worked then and it works now.

Then I didn't know anything about what *really* whining meant. Nor did I know anything about consequences. Now I do. When my first husband, David, a Navy test pilot, was tragically killed in a crash, I quickly found out what it *really* meant to *really* have something to whine about.

Somehow I survived, but only because of my best friend, Jane. We had become fast friends when fate found us buying new homes next door to each other back in 1968. We were pioneers in a newly suburbanized area north of Los Angeles called Westlake Village, The City in The Country.

Jane and I had a lot in common. I knew immediately that we were a perfect match the day our new carpets were installed. Jane's floor covering was lime green while I had chosen bright orange. Remember, it was the dawning of the Age of Aquarius. We were determined that our homes would be psychedelically correct. We weren't just California dreaming, we were California living.

Despite the ray of sunlight Jane's friendship provided, David was dead and, frankly, I wished I were, too. My babies missed their daddy. We all did. My first year of widowhood was tough, but Jane ushered me through it by being my one and only guest at a yearlong pity party. Jane knew a lot about whining since she had survived an incredibly tragic childhood. She stepped up to the table with innovative, cutting edge whining techniques that she generously shared with me.

For instance, Jane knew all about looking vulnerable and helpless. She had the biggest, saddest eyes in the world. Together we had the best pity party imaginable. It consisted of a few martinis and lots of commiserating, followed by lots of laughing, and it went on evening after evening. We functioned well during the day knowing happy hour was coming.

Then one day, I was finally all talked and cried out. Jane made me go out to mark the occasion. It was Christmas time. She forced me to go to a party. I resisted but she insisted. Friends don't let friends whine forever. At that party, I met my second husband. Jane was my matron of honor at our wedding and again at our twenty-fifth anniversary. At that point, we put our pity parties on hiatus for many years while various personal developments took us away from each other. They started up again when Jane got divorced, and then found out she had Stage-3 colon cancer. Now our roles were reversed. She talked while I listened. It was her turn to be angry. It was my turn to listen with unconditional love.

Our final pity party lasted for three years, during which she fought the cancer. We had some of our best times during these years. When I would spend the nights with her at the hospital, we would try not to cry, but laugh instead. It felt so good just to be together at our own private slumber party that laughing came naturally, in fluid waves. It helped us both to relive and recount all of our old, fun times. Our sweet silliness helped to make the long nights shorter.

I was devastated when I lost my best friend. It really hit me hard on the first March 12th after she was gone. My husband, David had died on that day. It was the first time in thirty-two years that Jane hadn't called me to see how I was doing on that anniversary. She was the only one who always remembered. It had always been a tough day for me, but now it was even tougher without Jane. I still miss her so much that I haven't removed her from my cell phone speed dial list, just in case.

Aside from helping us get through major tragedies, whining can also accomplish many other wonderful things. Whining works because it gets you attention. It can get what you want or may need. Also, whining is an avenue for communicating that lets you bond with family or friends. As Jane and I proved, it can be very therapeutic. It is important to reach out to others. It can't hurt but it could help.

After the whining dies down, you will find solutions that will replace the sorrow. Companions can become conduits of compassion. They will help you to make a new plan, an aggressive attack on whatever ails you. It just takes a steady pace of one step at a time, with no looking back. Your best friends will help you face the truth when you can't do it yourself, and listen to your stories no matter how sad they get—while at the same time making you laugh. With your best friend along for the ride, anything is possible. Just ask Lucy and Ethel or Jane and January.

**A good friend is a connection to life,
a tie to the past, a road to the future,
the key to sanity in a totally insane world.**

—Lois Wyse

Chapter Eleven

Grandparents

The other day, one of my dear friends asked me, "If you had to do it all over again, would you have children?" I didn't even have to think before responding immediately, "No, No, No and No!" I repeated it four times because we have four children and I didn't want to leave anyone out, thus leaving myself open to accusations of favoritism...again, again, again and again. I've been there and done that. My friend, who has wisely chosen to raise animals instead of kids, loved my answer so much that she had to ask me, "Why?"

Jokingly, I told her that if I had to do it all over again, "I'd skip the children and go straight to the grandchildren." It's a fun answer and not too far from the truth; plus, if you don't like what grandkids say or do when they're with you, then you can give them back to their parents.

It's quite simple. Everyone knows that having grandchildren is your reward for not killing your own children. The best part about having grandchildren is all the wonderful things that they say that are so pure, so unfiltered and so true.

For example, my four-year-old grandson and I were talking one day about our favorite things in life. I told him that he was one of my favorite things. He thought about it for a while, and then out of the blue said, "Mor Mor, did you know that my favorite things are Power Rangers and Big Boobies?"

I hadn't been aware of these preferences before, but I am now, and I also now know for a fact that he's definitely his grandfather's grandson.

My kids have always said the funniest things but without a doubt, my grandchildren are even funnier. Obviously, they have inherited their grandparents' senses of humor, our playfulness and our ability to ignore their parents.

The fact that grandchildren and their grandparents share a common enemy helps to keep them close. Also, it helps that we are all very good at keeping secrets. When we have to deal with their parents, it's best to stick with the "don't ask, don't tell" policy. In other words, what happens at Grandma's *stays* at Grandma's! We try not to whine out loud about anything in front of our grandchildren ever because we know that any kid no matter how loyal can "narc" on you at anytime. That's when you send them back right away.

When it comes to whining grandparents, the equation is simple and constant: Grandchildren can't do anything wrong whereas their parents can't do anything right. Now that we've broken the code, it's easier to get through family dinners, holidays and vacations.

As for the following Grandparent whines, none of them apply to me or my husband. All our kids know that I'm simply a humble humorist trying to sell some books in order to beef up their inheritances.

> **The simplest toy,**
> **one which even the youngest child can operate,**
> **is called a grandparent.**
>
> —*Sam Levenson*

Top Ten
Grandparents' Whines

#1 Time and Distance
#2 Manners
#3 Respect
#4 Naps and Bedtime
#5 Discipline
#6 Food and Eating
#7 Parents
#8 Potty Training
#9 Clothes and Hair
#10 Babysitting

Have children while your parents are still young
enough to take care of them.

—*Rita Rudner*

1
Time and Distance

An hour with your grandchildren can make you feel young again.
Anything longer than that, and you start to age quickly.

—Gene Perret

Whine A: It's their parent's fault that...

...our grandchildren live so far away.

Why: As a grandparent, time is always running out, and any time spent with your grandchildren immediately become some of the best times in your life. Unfortunately, so many grandchildren live so very far away that we don't see enough of them. The distance seems greater and greater the older we get. They start to grow up and don't have time for anyone except their friends. Generally, they hate their parents but seem to love their grandparents, so we don't have all that much to whine about, actually.

Whine B: We never get to see them.

Cure: The "**family cruise**" cure is the almost perfect solution for our family. We could be going on a cruise to Hades and if we're paying for them, too, they all want to go. I don't know if it's the running wild all over the ship with cousins or the unlimited soft ice cream, but grandkids love cruising, too. It's perfect because everyone does their own thing in their own time. We only eat together once a day, at dinner; and once a day is more than enough for a family of fourteen to sit down anywhere together, let alone in a formal dining room on a ship.

2
Manners

> When grandparents enter the door,
> discipline flies out the window.
>
> —*Ogden Nash*

Whine A: It's their parent's fault that...

...our grandchildren act like that.

Why: Grandparents don't whine about their grandchildren's lack of manners but rather what a horrible job their parents are doing raising them. It's never the kids' fault, but always the parents'. Most grandchildren know this and will act up just to remind Granny that their parents are falling down on the job. I'm aware that this may sound like I'm saying that the grandchild is always right and that their parents are always wrong. Well, it sounds like that because that's exactly what I *am* saying.

Whine B: Don't even think about it.

Cure: Grandchildren love going through the "**Please and Thank-you etiquette Boot Camp**" cure with their grandparents. It's amazing how quickly their manners shape up under the tutelage of their patient and doting grandparents—especially on the way to Chuck E. Cheese or Six Flags. If this doesn't work, the brownie bribe will work wonders with the most willful child. This will most likely be the child who acts the most like his or her parent—remember, the little darling who put you through parenthood Hell all those years ago?

3
Respect

**There was no respect for youth when I was young,
and now that I am old, there is no respect for age—
I missed it coming and going.**

—J.B. Priestly

Whine A: It's their parent's fault that...

...our grandchildren have no respect.

Why: There doesn't seem to be as much time for anything these days, which leaves even less time than ever for such low-priority directives as respecting your elders. In our 24/7 Internet world, everything is taking place at such an incredible rate of speed that our grandchildren are missing out on old fashioned values. There doesn't seem to be even enough time to teach them about country, flag and honor let alone standing up and opening up doors for those who have come before them.

Whine B: ...and not for the better.

Cure: We always try to make the time to take our grandchildren with us every **"Memorial Day"** to the services at our local veterans' cemetery. It sounds morbid, but it is always a festive, fun day with the traditional flags, music and dramatic fly-over of fighter jets in the "missing man" formation. We see our friends and neighbors while paying our respects to the bravest of the brave and teaching our grandchildren the importance of each act. Their BaBa, who is a real live war hero, even shares some benign stories from his Army days. It reminds all of us that cemeteries don't have to be sad, but can engender fun and fond memories.

158

4
Naps and Bedtimes

Two things I dislike about my granddaughter – when she won't take her afternoon nap, and when she won't let me take mine.

—*Gene Perret*

Whine A: *It's their parent's fault that...*

...there's no schedule.

Why: For some reason, my grandchildren's generation has not been taught about the sacredness of naptime or the sanctity of an early bedtime. Now it seems that kids just fall asleep wherever and whenever they happen to drop down for the count. I see them all over the place, roaming around exhausted and cranky while making everyone else miserable in the process. This phenomenon is especially prevalent around dinnertime in most families, or when the grandparents are visiting.

Whine B: Why can't they *make* them nap?

Cure: The only way to deal with the disappearing naptime and bedtime routine is by utilizing the **"totally ignore it"** cure. It doesn't pay to protest because no one is listening, least of all the parents or grandkids. This is a difficult thing for some grandparents, like my husband, to accept. You must try to remember that it's not your problem and life is too short to make it so. Soon the parents will not be going to bed either. They'll be waiting up all night for the kids to get home. Sweet payback!

5
Discipline

> What children need most are the essentials
> that grandparents provide in abundance.
> They give unconditional love, kindness,
> patience, humor, comfort, lessons in life.
> And, most importantly, cookies.
>
> —*Rudolph Giuliani*

Whine A: It's their parents' fault that...

...they run wild.

Why: These days it seems like most parents are terrified of their children. I think it must be the influence from all the television that we let them watch while they were growing up, though I couldn't pinpoint a source for their parental terror. It certainly wasn't our fault because we certainly weren't afraid of them. They all seem to think that life should be like TV, or their children will hate them. Actually it gets down to the simple fact that our grandchildren are all much, much brighter than their parents. Consequently, they get to run the show. It makes sense to me.

Whine B: Don't even think it.

Cure: As grandparents, we especially enjoy sharing with our grandkids the **"they may let you get away with it at home but not here"** cure. If they are bright, they will know exactly what you mean when you say it, and respect you for it, too. Sadly, the parents haven't a clue. It is unfortunate, but it doesn't spoil our fun and games. We love being the stern but benevolent dictators, and they humor us, which is just the way we all like it.

6
Food and Eating

**If God had intended us to follow recipes,
He wouldn't have given us grandmothers.**

—Linda Henley

Whine A: It's their parent's fault that ...

...they don't eat properly.

Why: Ours is a world with so much going on that there isn't enough time to eat a proper meal, let alone prepare it from fresh ingredients in your own kitchen. Most families have two income-earning adults who take turns picking up fast food or take out. I know it isn't fair to blame the parents for everything, but who else is there? It certainly isn't our grandchildren's fault that they demand junk food and get it. Besides, Mor-Mor told them that chocolate is the new broccoli.

Whine B: Why can't they cook a real meal?

Cure: When you don't know what to do or why something stupid regarding food is happening between your kids and their kids, it is best to utilize the **"do nothing, say nothing"** cure. Always remain careful not to criticize the parents in front of the grandkids. You can, however, make a few subtle suggestions, especially if it is your DNA daughter in the kitchen. Do not under any circumstances criticize the in-law parent. If you do, be sure it is while you are on your way out the door. Remember it's really no big deal because the grandkids will be at your door soon, eager to find all the really good junk food. You are what you eat, especially if it's a sweet treat.

7
Parents

The reason grandchildren and grandparents get along so well is that they have a common enemy.

—*Sam Levenson*

Whine A: It's their parent's fault because...

...they don't know what they're doing.

Why: It's just easier to blame or criticize parents for everything and save the praise for the grandkids. The parents are always getting in the way of our fun with all sorts of silly rules. You know, the ones about early bedtimes and sensible meals. Really, what's so wrong with pop tarts and ice cream for breakfast?

Whine B: They should know better.

Cure: It is easier on everyone to **"send the parents off on a long holiday"** so you can be alone with the grandkids. Everyone knows that the little darlings are perfectly behaved when they are with you. Besides, the kids sense the fear in their parents and know how to take advantage of it. Grandparents, on the other hand, are fearless, and so much more fun—because they know the kids will eventually be going home with their parents.

8
Potty Training and Binkies

If nothing is going well, call BaBa and MorMor.

—Norwegian Proverb

Whine A: It's their parent's fault that...

...they aren't trained yet.

Why: Today's parents seem to be afraid of toilet training their kids or taking their binkies away from them even though they know they must if their children are ever to evolve. No one even thinks of training these days until they are three years old. The only reason most of them get trained is that the nursery school won't take them in diapers. I can't figure it out. We trained our kids early for everything. It probably made them all too neurotic to train their own kids in the same fashion. But even if it was our fault originally, it's more fun to blame the parents now. Who on earth would still be changing poopy diapers on a three year old besides our kids?

Whine B: Don't you want to be a big boy/girl?

Cure: For potty training, I advocate the chocolate-based "**M&M's or Hersheys Kisses**" cure. In some of life's situations, bribery is the only answer, and if you can get them trained with a few well-placed bribes in order to calm your own nerves, then it will be well worth it. If they don't like chocolate, then they need to get into therapy as soon as possible. For binkies, you just cut the tip off slowly one day at a time until the binkie simply disappears. My granddaughter handed it back to me and said, "It's broken. I don't want it anymore."

9
Clothes and Hair

> **A grandmother pretends she doesn't know who you are on Halloween.**
>
> —*Erma Bombeck*

Whine A: It's their parent's fault that ...

...they look like orphans.

Why: Kids today adore dressing like punk rockers, hip hoppers or teen queens. For them, life is like a great big costume party. The issue here is that they all want to dress just like their friends or the people they see on television. As for the hair, this has been going on since time began. Everyone alive has had a ridiculous hair moment—especially their parents. It goes with the territory.

Whine B: How can they let them look like this?

Cure: I adore dressing up, too, so for us and the grandkids, life really is like one great big "**Halloween costume party**" cure. Most kids know it drives their parents crazy when they are dressed like rappers or drama teen queens, and most grandparents are happy to assist in this exercise. As for the hair, what can *we* say? Ba Ba had a perm and Mor Mor got her hair braided into cornrows on her Caribbean vacation cruise, so we have no room to criticize anyone else's coiffing decisions. The important thing here is to be sure to take lots and lots of pictures. How else can your family treasure these precious moments in time once they've passed?

10
Babysitting

> **Grandparents are there to help the child
> get into mischief
> they haven't thought of yet.**
>
> —*Gene Perret*

Whine A: It's their parent's fault because...

...they don't call on us enough.

Why: Babysitting can be a blessing or a burden depending on who you are and how your grandkids act when they are with you. They can either use you too much or not enough. No one likes to be taken for granted, so it is important to have a protocol for babysitting grandkids. It is best to set the ground rules from the day they come home from the hospital; otherwise, all concerned may encounter problems at some later, poorly scheduled and managed date. Waving good-bye to Mommy and Daddy should be a fun experience, especially when there are cookies in the pantry.

Whine B: I wish they used us more.

Cure: Wow, **the parents are gone and it's fun time**! We adore the time we get to spend alone with our grandkids, but we do have our rules. They want to know that someone is in control besides them. Grandkids are used to controlling their parents, so it is a nice break for them to let us take charge. If you approach it correctly, babysitting can be a blast. If you stay up too late playing, the grandkids can sleep it off on the ride home while you do the same as soon as they walk out the door. It's the perfect arrangement.

Best Overall Remedy
for Whining Grandparents

The Three Hour Cure

All grandparents whine about the same things. Their grandchildren are either too far away or too close. They either don't see enough of them or they see too much of them. These are the basic whines of grandparents, ranking right up there with social security, health care, fixed income, sexual dysfunction and a newfound dependence on Depends.

I have devised the Three Hour Cure for NaNa and PaPa. This involves always living about three hours driving time away from your grandchildren. Three hours is too long a drive to just drop by yet long enough to force a telephone call before initiating a visit. And it is too long a trip not to find anyone home when you get there.

Under the effects of this cure, no party gets to take any other party for granted or take advantage of said party in any way–and remember, you're always close enough in case anyone has to be returned to sender. This distance puts a halt to the proverbial surprise morning visits that grandparents often receive, with little people being dropped off in their pajamas.

This cure is especially effective for grandparents who love having sleepovers because the parents are more inclined to let the kids spend the night rather than drive three hours to pick them up. All grandparents and grandkids know that the fun really begins once Dad's rear car lights are out of sight. Without any grownups around to spoil the fun, we can start enjoying our cookies and Cokes. It's so special when we can have our super silly secret sleepovers.

"The greatest gift you can give your grandchildren is to grow old gracefully." I came up with this motto in my fifties, before I started to whine about getting old. It's so important for grandparents to set a good example and try to be winners instead of whiners. Little pitchers not only have big ears; they are also born mimics. They can do what you do and say what you say exactly as you did, especially if you don't want it repeated in public.

Despite an occasional moan or groan, grandchildren know that their grandparents love watching them more than television. NaNa is MaMa with Oreo cookies and hugs. PaPa is DaDa with big laps and lots of quarters. In my case, I'd rather not even consider this ridiculous Three Hour Cure. Don't my kids know that we silly sausages always need to be close to our fellow silly sausages? For us, three hours is too long because we really can't bear to be separated by such a distance from our grandkids. Just don't tell their parents that.

Post Script
Win, Don't Whine

In case you haven't noticed, there truly is a whining epidemic taking place. The reason for this epidemic is that, as I did when my first husband died, the U.S. received "something to *really* whine about" with 9/11, the Iraqi war and all the turmoil that followed.

Prior to 9/11, the saddest thing I had ever experienced was something my three-year-old daughter would do after my first husband's accidental death. Every night I would watch her sitting alone patiently, looking out the window and waiting for Daddy to come home. There she'd be with her pigtails and red shoes while her baby sister was napping. When I'd ask what she was doing, she'd say, "Oh, nothing. Just looking out the window."

She was trying to be brave while pretending and hoping that he'd come back. She desperately wanted us to be happy and laugh again. She didn't want Mommy to be so sad. It broke my heart to see her hoping, yet knowing he was gone forever from our lives.

9/11 gave me the same feeling. I watched the families waiting and hoping they'd see their loved ones walking through the door. We were all hoping, yet knowing they weren't coming back. Our life as we had known it was over forever. Our hearts ached for them and for us. We wanted it to be nothing but a bad dream.

It wasn't. For my generation, the JFK assassination, the Vietnam carnage, the Challenger crash, 9/11 and the *déjà vu* of the Iraqi war are our worst collective nightmares. They are the bad dreams that haunt us. Furthermore, it's not a pretty picture ahead that we're facing. It won't be easy, but I feel that we can make some changes to the landscape. A lot of headway can be made if we try to use humor and hope to make things a little better.

I don't claim to have all the answers, but I do have a few ideas. I'm not the Whine Tester for nothing, nor did I become a self-proclaimed expert on all sorts of things like chocolate and whining just to have some fun on my radio show. Like everyone else, I want to make a difference. People need to know that we can and we must have some fun while making some really important suggestions to all the other silly sausages in the world.

What's a silly sausage? If you have to ask, then I'm really worried about you. Our grandbabies came up with that term for the people in their lives whose sweet silliness makes life so wonderful.

Life is wonderful because the reality is that we are entering the awakening of a new age. I am announcing the arrival of "The Advent of Venting." Don't worry! It has nothing to do with getting ready for Lent or fasting.

It's the beginning of a new era for mankind. Suddenly, it has become morally and socially correct to tell the truth about things that have been so wrong for so long. For the sake of our heirs, honesty is not only the best policy, it will be the only policy. Finally we can tell the truth. Whether it's about a lousy war, sexuality, corrupt government, healthcare, corporate greed, gay marriages, civil rights, lost pensions, extremism or terrorism, the time has come to vent and let it out.

Mind you, there is a big difference between whining and venting. Whining is something that we do only to express our unhappiness about a situation, not to process it. Whining can have a negative effect whereas venting can have a positive one. Venting can help you to dredge up and release your angers, resentments and frustrations—far more powerful emotions than are often dealt with effectively through whining.

You may ask, "How can you tell the difference between whining and venting for sure?" That's easy! Try to remember that whining is like slowly simmering and steaming about something while venting is like exploding and letting off steam. One is internal combustion and the other is external combustion. One is harmful and one is healthy. One is toxic waste and the other is a healing tonic for happiness.

If you find that someone continues to whine incessantly despite opportunities for healthy venting, you might try following this very ancient tribal cure, which resembles a sort of positive venting experience:

In ancient times, it was the practice of some of the tribes to deal with punishment in a very unique way. When a member of the tribe committed a wrong, the entire tribe would gather in a circle with the offending person sitting in the middle. Then one of the elders would recite the offense and the reason it was unacceptable to the tribal community.

That out of the way, each member of the circle would be allowed to speak to the offending person. One by one, they would make a comment or tell a story that would praise that person, literally bombarding the offender with every good thing or compliment they could come up with that could possibly build up the wrongdoer's self-esteem. They would tell stories of past accomplishments or good works; no good deed would be forgotten or go unmentioned. This session would end with everyone embracing that person with love and forgiveness.

Now, this is my idea of positive reinforcement, and a universal cure for every person and most situations. Because this cure is ageless and timeless, there is no reason why this same technique cannot be applied to the tribes people who are the whiners in our midst. When they start to whine in order to complain or get attention, turn it around by bombarding them with positive vibrations. Try it! You'll like it.

And if that doesn't work, bombard them with chocolate...lots and lots of it.

Now you have a plan that will turn any whiner into a winner. It's up to you to take a stand and make a statement, being creative and constructive. Do something. Do anything. You can make a difference. If you don't do it, who will? You need to do more with your life than kick back and zone out on Comedy Central, which is so easy to do.

Remember, I will be cheering for every one of you and hoping to hear from you soon. Besides, if you don't do something or keep in touch, the Whine Tester will come back to haunt you. Just ask the little girl who was sitting and waiting at the window so long, long ago.

Before I say good-bye, remember to take your vitamins, dress warm, wear clean underwear and always know that there is a mother who loves you—somewhere—very much. Yes, you and all the other silly sausages in the world.

To chart your own progress, following is a helpful set of instructions that will clearly delineate the differences between whiners and winners for you on a number of typically whine-producing issues:

Whiners would say the weather is...
too hot, too cold, too humid, too dry, too wet, too windy, too icy, too snowy, too cloudy or too foggy!

Winners would say the weather is...
sunny, fair, pleasant, gorgeous, clear, fabulous, lovely, invigorating, terrific, mysterious or bright!

Whiners would say food is...
too hot, too cold, too sweet, too sour, too spicy, too overcooked, too undercooked, too much, too little or too awful!

Winners would say food is...
good, tasty, plentiful, nutritious, festive, beautiful, bountiful, healthy, interesting, sweet or...chocolate!

Whiners would say sex is...
too much, too little, too fast, too slow, too long, too predictable, too unromantic, too boring, too short or too kinky!

Winners would say sex is...
Spontaneous, intimate, enjoyable, mutual, fun, relaxing, fulfilling, innovative, creative or frequent!

Whiners would say bodies are...
too fat, too thin, too heavy, too light, too flabby, too plump, too skinny, too short, too tall or too chunky!

Winners would say bodies are...
healthy, active, toned, energetic, fit, fabulous, durable, attractive, pain-free or firm!

Whiners would say spouses are...
too expensive, too cheap, too needy, too selfish, too boring, too controlling, too demanding, too nagging, too messy or too neat!

Winners would say spouses are.....
loving, understanding, cooperative, giving, creative, encouraging, independent, exciting or generous!

Whiners would say clothes are...
too tight, too loose, too trendy, too many,
too slutty, too expensive, too conservative, too hot,
too sheer or too dated!

Winners would say clothes are...
attractive, enjoyable, affordable, comfortable, fabulous,
fashionable, expressive, creative, original or trendy!

Whiners would say families are...
too demanding, too nosey, too expensive,
too needy, too whiney, too unappreciative,
too possessive, too noisy, too big or too much!

Winners would say families are.....
understanding, attentive, helpful, loving, caring, agreeable, helpful, sharing, giving or honest!

Whiners would say vacations are....
too expensive, too short, too long, too hectic,
too boring, too sea sick, too many kids, too many bugs, too little rest or too trying!

Winners would say vacations are.....
enjoyable, affordable, carefree, restful, fun, memorable, adventurous, unforgettable, exciting or unique!

Whiners would say holidays are...
too stressful, too expensive, too hectic, too tiring,
too many, too much shopping, too much entertaining, too much
cooking, too fattening...
or just too much!

Winners would say holidays are...
delightful, wonderful, special, stress-free, festive,
joyful, fabulous, fulfilling, generous or loving!

Whiners would say governments are...
too expensive, too undemocratic, too corrupt,
too political, too big, too self-serving, too devious,
too inflationary, too wealthy or too inept!

Winners would say governments are... compassionate, understanding,
responsible, wise, fair, representative, cooperative, creative, helpful
or honest!

**If people behaved like governments
you'd call the cops.**

—*Kelvin Throop*

Appendix

Woe is Me...
I'm a Celebrity

Celebrities must be the luckiest people in the world, but you wouldn't know that by listening to the way some of them whine. Television is filled with Tele-babies who have turned whining into a credible art form. Stephen Colbert of Comedy Central and Joy Behar of *The View* along with Regis Philbin and Joan Rivers, the King and Queen of Whining, lead the way in this respect, having groomed themselves to be able to whine—and whine big—about anything on topic, from politics to the most miniscule of daily annoyances—Philbin's specialty. This kind of whining can be very funny and cathartic, and when it comes down to it, it's all done in the name of comedy and good fun.

Then there's another type of celebrity whining—the kind about how it's so hard to be a celebrity. These are the people we love to hate. They are the ones you just want to slap, saying, "Give me a break." These are the celebrities who act like big brats, the spoiled rotten ones we see and hear about everyday. Despite their good fortune, they just can't stop from being big, belly-aching babies. For some, their fondest dreams have become their biggest nightmares. To us, their complaints are nothing short of ridiculous.

On the following pages are some of my favorite "Cele-Bratty" quotes, along with my responses, which I hope will cure these coddled crybabies for once and for all!

✿ ✿ ✿ ✿ ✿
"Oh, God, I struggle with self-esteem all the time!
I think everyone does.
I have so much wrong with me, it's unbelievable."
Angelina Jolie

Not to Jennifer Aniston.

✿ ✿ ✿ ✿ ✿
"Fame is a bitch, man!"

"I'm one of those people you hate
because of genetics. It is the truth."

Brad Pitt

Most men would love your problems and your wife!

✿ ✿ ✿ ✿ ✿
"If somebody ever wished to be me for a day,
they'd be the most pissed off person.
They would be, like, in hell."
Jennifer Aniston

**Aside from Angelina,
most women would love your problems!**

✿ ✿ ✿ ✿ ✿
"I'm really white trash."
"I'm the flavor of the month."
George Clooney

Most conservatives would agree.

✿ ✿ ✿ ✿ ✿

"Face it. I didn't become famous until I took my clothes off."
Jude Law

Now that you're famous, you can leave them on.

✿ ✿ ✿ ✿ ✿

"The very thought of a diet, makes me want chips and ice cream.
And I just hate going to the gym. I cannot stand it."
Keira Knightly

Me too!

✿ ✿ ✿ ✿ ✿

"I'm shy, paranoid, whatever word you want to use.
I hate fame. I've done everything I can to avoid it."
Johnny Depp

How about stop making movies?

✿ ✿ ✿ ✿ ✿

"Just standing around looking beautiful is boring."
Michelle Pfeiffer

I'm so sorry! Looking like you must be a drag!

✿ ✿ ✿ ✿ ✿

"I don't want to be known as the granddaughter of the Hiltons.
I want to be known as Paris."
Paris Hilton

How about as the actress who couldn't act?

✿ ✿ ✿ ✿ ✿

**"In Hollywood everything is so documented.
If you go out for a drink with somebody,
it's passed around the world so quickly."**
Catherine Zeta Jones

Duh!

✿ ✿ ✿ ✿ ✿

**"I don't think I realized that the cost of fame is that it's open
season on every moment of your life."**
Julia Roberts

Another sad story.

✿ ✿ ✿ ✿ ✿

**"Celebrity is a pretty stunning thing.
At first I was like 'They love me! Oh, I love them, too!'
And suddenly, I was tap dancing on my pedestal and it was
WHACK! Facedown in the dirt."**
Sharon Stone

Now, this is a gal who knows the score.

✿ ✿ ✿ ✿ ✿

"I don't want to be a personality."
Richard Gere

Sorry, it's a little too late for that.

✿ ✿ ✿ ✿ ✿

"I must say that I do wrestle with the amount of money I make, but at the end of the day what am I gonna say? I took less money so Rupert Murdock could have more?"

Tom Hanks

It's so hard to know what to do.

✿ ✿ ✿ ✿ ✿

"I'm not mad about my ankles, they're a little too skinny."

Jennifer Lopez

Forget the ankles. Baby, you've got back!

✿ ✿ ✿ ✿ ✿

"I want people to fall in love with my voice before my image."

Jessica Simpson

Sorry, not likely to happen.

✿ ✿ ✿ ✿ ✿

"I hate when people call me a teen queen."

Lindsay Lohan

Would out-of-control brat be better?

✿ ✿ ✿ ✿ ✿

"It stirs up envy, fame does. People feel fame gives them some kind of privilege to walk up to you and say anything to you, and it won't hurt your feelings, like it's happening to your clothing."

Marilyn Monroe

Forget about the clothing!
Most men just wanted to see you without clothes.

✿ ✿ ✿ ✿ ✿
"It's like kissing Hitler."
Tony Curtis about Marilyn Monroe

JFK didn't think so.

✿ ✿ ✿ ✿ ✿
**"The worst part of success is to try to find
someone who is happy for you."**
Bette Midler

How about the ones who are in your will?

✿ ✿ ✿ ✿ ✿
**"Being a celebrity is probably the closest to being a
beautiful woman as you can get."**
Kevin Costner

Being a beautiful woman doesn't pay as well.

✿ ✿ ✿ ✿ ✿
**"Trying not to be a dick takes work,
and there are times when I'm not good at it."**
George Clooney

**Women don't care what you work at
as long as they can watch you do it.**

✿ ✿ ✿ ✿ ✿
**"One thing about being successful is that I stopped being afraid of
dying. Once you're a star, you're dead already. You're embalmed."**
Dustin Hoffman

**If you're already dead,
why does it look like you're having so much fun?**

✿ ✿ ✿ ✿ ✿
"Fame sorta destroys everything you love,
people don't realize that."
George Clooney

Good news:
Your villa on Lake Como is still standing.

✿ ✿ ✿ ✿ ✿
"Success is like death. The more successful you become, the
higher the houses in the hills get and the higher the fences get."
Kevin Spacey

Just try living in the flatlands.

✿ ✿ ✿ ✿ ✿
"It's a tough thing. You get in a situation where you feel you have
to be perfect all the time and it sucks."
Leonardo DiCaprio

Try being in a situation that's never perfect.

✿ ✿ ✿ ✿ ✿
"I'm sick of being known as the sexy guy that writes great songs."
Tom DeLonge

You're safe with people over fifty.
Believe me, they've never heard of you.

✿ ✿ ✿ ✿ ✿
"Just because I have my standards, they think I'm bitch."
Diana Ross

Now why would that be?

✿ ✿ ✿ ✿ ✿

"Being a sex symbol is a heavy load to carry,
especially when one is tired, hurt and bewildered."
Marilyn Monroe

Sometimes what we wish for isn't so great!

✿ ✿ ✿ ✿ ✿

"Just because you like my stuff doesn't mean I owe you anything."
Bob Dylan

Who ever said that you do?

✿ ✿ ✿ ✿ ✿

"People hate me because I am multifaceted, talented wealthy,
internationally famous genius."
Jerry Lewis

Well, so much for modesty.

✿ ✿ ✿ ✿ ✿

"A man has to be Joe McCarthy to be called ruthless. All a
woman has to do is put you on hold."
Marlo Thomas

Try being a woman without a famous father.

✿ ✿ ✿ ✿ ✿

"There is not one female comic
who was beautiful as a little girl."
Joan Rivers

Their mothers would disagree.

❖ ❖ ❖ ❖ ❖

"The more you stay in this job, the more you realize that a public figure, a major public figure, is a lonely man."

Richard Nixon

Too bad you weren't just a minor public figure.

❖ ❖ ❖ ❖ ❖

"I'd rather be dead than singing 'Satisfaction' when I'm forty-five."

Mick Jagger

So what happened?

❖ ❖ ❖ ❖ ❖

"Finishing second in the Olympics gets you silver. Finishing second in politics gets you oblivion."

Richard Nixon

Unless, you are impeached.

❖ ❖ ❖ ❖ ❖

"I don't mind that I'm fat. You still get the same money."

Marlon Brando

What about all of us who had to look at you?

❖ ❖ ❖ ❖ ❖

"Most of the time I don't have much fun. The rest of the time I don't have any fun at all."

Woody Allen

Have you tried people your own age?

✿ ✿ ✿ ✿ ✿
"The average dog is nicer than the average person."
Andy Rooney

What about the average cat?

✿ ✿ ✿ ✿ ✿
**"I have the feeling that when my ship comes in
I'll be at the airport."**
Charles M. Schultz

It's better than being in the subway.

✿ ✿ ✿ ✿ ✿
"I guess I look like a rock quarry that someone has dynamited."
Charles Bronson

It's better than looking like a cesspool.

✿ ✿ ✿ ✿ ✿
"Spring makes everything look dirty."
Katherine Whitehorn

Because it is!

✿ ✿ ✿ ✿ ✿
"I have eyes like those of a dead pig."
Marlon Brando

And your point is?

✿ ✿ ✿ ✿ ✿

"The only parts of my original body are my elbows."
Phyllis Diller

What about your mouth?

✿ ✿ ✿ ✿ ✿

"I get so tired listening to one million dollars here, one million dollars there, it's so petty."
Imelda Marcos

Girl, you need to go shopping.

✿ ✿ ✿ ✿ ✿

"I never set out to hurt anybody deliberately unless it was, you know important. Like a league game or something."
Dick Butkus

He sounds like the Mother Teresa of pro-football.

✿ ✿ ✿ ✿ ✿

"I'm not conceited. Conceit is a fault and I have no faults."
David Lee Roth

What does your ex-wife say?

✿ ✿ ✿ ✿ ✿

"My movies are the kind they show in prisons and airplanes, because nobody can leave."
Burt Reynolds

They could escape or jump out!

❁ ❁ ❁ ❁ ❁

"I haven't committed a crime.
What I did was fail to comply with the law."
David Dinkins

Try telling that to the judge.

❁ ❁ ❁ ❁ ❁

"I don't care what is written about me so long as it isn't true."
Katherine Hepburn

It won't be.

❁ ❁ ❁ ❁ ❁

"If people screw me, I screw back in spades."
Donald Trump

Just ask Rosie!

❁ ❁ ❁ ❁ ❁

About the Author

January Jones, The Whine Tester, is the self-proclaimed world's foremost expert on How to Stop Whining. She is a reformed whiner who lives every day in the No Whine Zone. Her credentials as a Whine-ologist known for dispensing clever and cute cures for whining come from her years as a woman, a wife, a widow, a mother and a grandmother. She is a weekly radio talk show host on *Thou Shalt Not Whine*, which airs on BigMediaUSA.com. The Whine Tester is featured on Fresh Talk, Amazing Women, Financial Freedom and as The Chocolate Expert on The Expert Channel.

Ms. Jones is a published author who has made over 500 media and personal appearance to promote her theories. She is a humorist who specializes in homemaker humor and an outrageous gal who loves sharing her theories, cures and conclusions. In 1998, Ms. Jones formed P. J. Publishing, named in honor of all women who like to work in their pajamas.

January Jones had a traditional parochial education and was raised in a normal, typical dysfunctional family. She became a stewardess and then married a Navy test pilot. They had two young daughters who were ages three and six weeks when she became a widow at 25 after her husband was killed in a test flight.

This was a traumatic turning point in January's life. Her husband had survived Vietnam while half of his squadron had not come home. She thought they were safe, but she and her two children soon found out that life can change in one instant.

Later, three became four when January married another pilot, Buckeye Leif (a Norwegian from Ohio, and Three-Star Pillow Whiner). They have been married close to forty years, and together they have four children and six grandchildren.

Early settlers of the southern California suburbs, they have lived in the Westlake Village area since 1968. For twenty years, they owned and managed the Thousand Oaks Racquet Club, which gave January the perfect opportunity to deal with whiners *and* winners on a daily basis. She reports that her experiences at the Racquet Club instilled in her the value of humor in difficult situations.

Using this philosophy, along with a lot of chocolate, January and Leif have shared more adventures in one lifetime than they ever could have imagined possible. Of course, if January were to share all of them with you here, she would have to kill you.

Because she is a woman and thus loves jewelry, she has created a promotional pin for her "Are you a Winner or a Whiner campaign?" The pin is an original design, shaped like a teardrop with a smile in the middle, and is also magnetized. Every morning you start out wearing it as a "Winner" with a smile for the world, but if at any time during the day you start whining, it must immediately be turned upside down. Now you are officially a "Whiner," with a grumpy face for the world to see.

The good news is that each day you can start all over as a winner. The pins are a humorous way to remind people to stop whining. They come in different colors for easy outfit coordination, and can even be worn as earrings. January's husband uses his as a ball marker when he plays golf. It's always a topic of conversation, since there are a lot of golfers who have been known to whine.

If you'd like to wear one of January's "Whiner/Winner" pins or give one as a gift to your favorite whiner or winner please go to:

www.thoushaltnotwhinehome.com.

You can sign on with your name and e-mail and you will be able to order as many pins as you need to share with others and spread the message:

Thou Shalt Not Whine!

Acknowledgments

I must begin by acknowledging Steve and Bill Harrison and their wonderful staff at Radio Television Interview Report. This book began as an idea and quickly became a reality due to my involvement in The Quantum Leap Program at RTIR.

The learning curve has been amazing. My book went from a simple manuscript with a lousy title, weak format and not much humor to a book that I am proud to publish and promote.

The Harrison boys do an incredibly good year-long mentoring program. Steve is especially effective with his honest and constructive criticism, cures and magnificent mentoring.

I would like to thank all my survey participants, especially Nancy Gatch, who provided me with invaluable teenager surveys. My family and friends were all so supportive, and it has been a joy to share this journey with them.

The staff at Beaufort Books headed by Eric Kampmann, along with Margot Atwell and Erin Smith, have been so creative and helpful with this entire project. Also, Vally Sharpe, our designer, who has created such a fun and delightful interior for our no whining adventure. Lastly, because he truly is the best, Rob Campbell, my brilliant editor, has helped me to reach out to whiners and winners everywhere with humor and hope.

Cheers & Chocolates,
January Jones

MORE Thou Shalt Not Whine

Share your favorite whines, cures and humorous quotes with the rest of the world. If you have a favorite quote (your own or someone else's) or a personal story about whining that you feel belongs in a future edition of *Thou Shalt Not Whine about Family, Holidays or The Whiner's Handbook from A to Z* , please send it to us.

January Jones
FAX 805-494-0051
To e-mail or visit our Web site:
Thoushaltnotwhine@hotmail.com
www.thoushaltnotwhinehome.com

You may use the following rubric for your submission(s), and we will make sure that you are credited for your contribution. Thank you.

Favorite Whine(s):

Favorite Whining Cure(s):

Favorite Whining Story(ies):

Favorite Quote(s) & Author(s):

Send Attachments To:

Thoushaltnotwhine@hotmail.com

All submissions become property of January Jones.

To contribute even further,
and possibly see your name in print:

Vent, Don't Whine
with
Pity Party Pals

Tell us about your Pity Party Pals and how they helped you through a difficult situation with love, laughter, humor and hope.

If you have ever been helped through a hard time by having a pity pal to vent to about a death, divorce, disease, drugs, drinking, disaster, dispute, dalliance, drama or disappointment and would like to share your experience with our readers, please submit your story to:

January Jones
FAX 805-494-0051
To e-mail or visit our Web site:

Pitypartypals@gmail.com
.
www.pitypartypals.com

We will make sure that you are credited for your contribution.
Thank you.

Note: All submissions become the property of January Jones.